THE HIGHLY SENSITIVE

How to Find Inner Peace, Develop Your Gifts, and Thrive

JUDY DYER

THE HIGHLY SENSITIVE:
How to Find Inner Peace, Develop Your Gifts, and Thrive
by Judy Dyer

© **Copyright 2018 by Judy Dyer**

All Rights Reserved.

Disclaimer: This book is designed to provide accurate and authoritative information in regard to the subject matter covered. By its sale, neither the publisher nor the author is engaged in rendering psychological or other professional services. If expert assistance or counseling is needed, the services of a competent professional should be sought.

ISBN-10: 1720622493
ISBN:13: 978-1720622499

ALSO BY JUDY DYER

*Empath: A Complete Guide for Developing Your Gift
and Finding Your Sense of Self*

*The Empowered Empath: A Simple Guide on Setting
Boundaries, Controlling Your Emotions, and Making Life Easier*

Empath and The Highly Sensitive: 2 Books in 1

Empaths and Narcissists: 2 Books in 1

*Narcissist: A Complete Guide for Dealing
with Narcissism and Creating the Life You Want*

*Narcissism: How to Stop Narcissistic Abuse,
Heal Your Relationships, and Transform Your Life*

*Anger Management: How to Take Control of Your Emotions
and Find Joy in Life*

CONTENTS

INTRODUCTION

In this guide, you will discover how to overcome the most common problems faced by Highly Sensitive Persons, or HSPs. You might be a little confused by the term "highly sensitive." In some places, being called "sensitive" is an insult, so you may be wondering whether it's a curse to be born an HSP. There's no denying that HSPs do face some big challenges—they are so much more sensitive than the world around them, after all! But, with the right guidance, you can make peace with your gift.

If you have always wondered why you seem somewhat different from those around you, learning about high sensitivity can come as a big relief. You aren't a freak, and you aren't deficient in any way. As you read through this book and learn more about HSPs, you'll come to realize how lucky you are to have been born with this gift! Many people would love to possess your empathy, appreciation of the fine arts, and capacity to ponder life's big questions.

It's well worth taking the time to understand your sensitive nature. Only then will you be able to lead a lifestyle that perfectly suits your needs. This book will help you take your first steps in coming to terms with your special trait.

In order to maximize the value you receive from this book, I highly encourage you to join our tight-knit community on Facebook. There you will be able to connect and share with other like-minded HSPs to continue your growth.

Taking this journey alone is not recommended, and this platform can provide an excellent support network for you.

It would be great to connect with you there,

Judy Dyer

To Join, Visit:
www.pristinepublish.com/hspgroup

DOWNLOAD THE AUDIO VERSION OF THIS BOOK FREE

If you love listening to audiobooks on the go or would enjoy a narration as you read along, I have great news for you. You can download the audio book version of *The Highly Sensitive* for FREE (Regularly $14.95) just by signing up for a FREE 30-day audible trial!

Visit: www.pristinepublish.com/audiobooks

YOUR FREE GIFT - HEYOKA EMPATH

A lot of empaths feel trapped, as if they've hit a glass ceiling they can't penetrate. They know there's another level to their gift, but they can't seem to figure out what it is. They've read dozens of books, been to counselling, and confided in other experienced empaths, but that glass ceiling remains. They feel alone, and alienated from the rest of the world because they know they've got so much more to give, but can't access it. Does this sound like you?

The inability to connect to your true and authentic self is a tragedy. Being robbed of the joy of embracing the full extent of your humanity is a terrible misfortune. The driving force of human nature is to live according to one's own sense of self, values, and emotions. Since the beginning of time, philosophers, writers, and scholars have argued that authenticity is one of the most important elements of an individual's well-being.

When there's a disconnect between a person's inner being and their expressions, it can be psychologically damaging. Heyokas are the most powerful type of empaths, and many of them are not fully aware of who they are. While other empaths experience feelings of overwhelm and exhaustion from absorbing others' energy and emotions, heyoka empaths experience an additional aspect of exhaustion in that they are fighting a constant battle with their inability to be completely authentic.

The good news is that the only thing stopping you from becoming your authentic self is a lack of knowledge. You need to know exactly who you are so you can tap into the resources that have been lying dormant within you. In this bonus e-book, you'll gain in-depth information about the seven signs that you're a heyoka empath, and why certain related abilities are such powerful traits. You'll find many of the answers to the questions you've been searching for your entire life such as:

- Why you feel uncomfortable when you're around certain people
- How you always seem to find yourself on the right path even though your decisions are not based on logic or rationale
- The reason you get so offended when you find out others have lied to you
- Why you analyze everything in such detail
- The reason why humor is such an important part of your life
- Why you refuse to follow the crowd, regardless of the consequences
- The reason why strangers and animals are drawn to you

There are three main components to authenticity: understanding who you are, expressing who you are, and letting the world experience who you are. Your first step on this journey is to know who you are, and with these seven signs that you're a heyoka empath, you'll find out. I've included snippets about the first three signs in this description to give you full confidence that you're on the right track:

Sign 1: You Feel and Understand Energy

Heyoka empaths possess a natural ability to tap into energy. They can walk into a room and immediately discern the atmosphere. When an individual walks past them, they can literally see into their soul because they can sense the aura that person is carrying. But empaths also understand their own energy, and they allow it to guide them. You will often hear this ability referred to as "the sixth sense." The general consensus is that only a few people have this gift. But the reality is that everyone was born with the ability to feel energy; it's just been demonized and turned into something spooky, when in actual fact, it's the most natural state to operate in.

Sign 2: You are Led by Your Intuition

Do you find that you just know things? You don't spend hours, days, and weeks agonizing over decisions, you can just feel that something is the right thing to do, and you go ahead and do it. That's because you're led by your intuition and you're connected to the deepest part of yourself. You know your soul, you listen to it, and you trust it. People like Oprah Winfrey, Steve Jobs and Richard Branson followed their intuition steadfastly and it led them to become some of the most successful people in the history of the world.

Living from within is the way we were created to be, and those who trust this ability will find their footing in life a lot more quickly than others. Think of it as a GPS system: when it's been programmed properly, it will always take you to your destination via the fastest route.

Sign 3: You Believe in Complete Honesty

In general, empaths don't like being around negative energy, and there's nothing that can shift a positive frequency faster than dishonesty. Anything that isn't the truth is a lie, even the tiny ones that we excuse away as "white lies." And as soon as they're released from someone's mouth, so is negative energy. Living an authentic life requires complete honesty at all times, and although the truth may hurt, it's better than not being able to trust someone. Heyoka empaths get very uncomfortable in the presence of liars. They are fully aware that the vibrations of the person don't match the words they are saying. Have you ever experienced a brain freeze mid-conversation? All of a sudden you just couldn't think straight, you couldn't articulate yourself properly, and things just got really awkward? That's because your empath antenna picked up on a lie.

Heyoka Empath: 7 Signs You're A Heyoka Empath & Why It's So Powerful is a revolutionary tool that will help you transition from uncertainty to complete confidence in who you are. In this easy-to-read guide, I will walk you through exactly what makes you a heyoka empath. I've done the research for you, so no more spending hours, days, weeks, and even years searching for answers, because everything you need is right here in this book.

You have a deep need to share yourself with the world, but you've been too afraid because you knew something was missing. The information within the pages of this book is the missing piece in the jigsaw puzzle of your life. There's no turning back now!

Get *Heyoka Empath* for Free by Visiting

www.pristinepublish.com/empathbonus

CHAPTER 1:

WHAT IS AN HSP, ANYWAY?

Have you always been told that you are too sensitive for your own good, that you need to "toughen up," or that you cry too easily? If you're a deep thinker who often feels as though you don't quite fit in, there's a good chance you might be an HSP.

This kind of sensitivity is more common than you might think. Dr. Elaine Aron, famous for her research with HSPs, states that approximately 20% of the population is highly sensitive.

SIGNS OF THE HIGHLY SENSITIVE PERSON – A HELPFUL LIST

How many of the following describe you?

1. A tendency to feel particularly overwhelmed in noisy environments

2. A preference for smaller gatherings of people rather than large crowds

3. A good track record of picking up on other people's moods and motives

4. An ability to notice little changes in the environment

5. A tendency to be easily moved by music, books, films, and other media

6. Heightened sensitivity to hunger, pain, medication, and caffeine

7. A need to recharge and relax alone on a regular basis

8. An appreciation of good manners and politeness

9. Difficulty in refusing others' requests for fear of hurting their feelings

10. Difficulty in forgiving yourself for even the smallest mistakes

11. Perfectionism and imposter syndrome

12. Trouble handling conflict and criticism

You don't have to answer "Yes!" to every item on this list to qualify as an HSP. Trust your intuition. If this list resonates with you, there's a good chance that you have a highly sensitive personality.

D.O.E.S. – A Useful Way to Think about High Sensitivity

The D.O.E.S. model is a helpful acronym that explains the HSP profile.

Depth of processing: HSPs have brains that work a little differently from the norm. They process incoming information—sights, sounds, smells, and so on—in a more thorough way. An HSP's mirror neurons—the cells in the brain that help us empathize with others—are more active than average. This explains why HSPs are especially sensitive to other people's moods and feelings and why they are readily overwhelmed in noisy places.

Overstimulation: Overstimulation is inevitable when you have a particularly sensitive brain! An HSP takes longer than the average person to process stimuli, so they soon become overwhelmed and drained in busy or crowded environments. This also accounts for their heightened sensitivity to pain and hunger.

Emotional reactivity: Emotional reactivity is probably what gets HSPs into trouble most often. They are always "tuned in" to their environment, so they cannot help but react strongly to both positive and negative situations. Unfortunately, their negative emotions can become all-consuming if not properly managed. Being so empathetic, they are also prone to picking up on other people's bad moods.

Sensing the subtle: HSPs do not have superhuman powers—they see and hear just about as well as anyone else. However, they do have a special ability to pick up on tiny details in the environment that other people usually miss.

For example, if you are an HSP, you may find that you are the first to notice when a vase of flowers has been moved to a different place in a room.

This attention to detail also applies in social settings. An HSP can easily identify deception and ulterior motives in a friend or partner. Even when someone tries to conceal their true nature, an HSP will usually be able to see through the act!

High sensitivity isn't a disorder or an illness, it's just a natural variation that occurs in a minority of the human population. An HSP is born possessing this trait, which cannot be learned or unlearned. Men are just as likely to be highly sensitive as women, so don't assume that you can't be an HSP if you are a man.

HSP MYTHS

High sensitivity isn't well understood. Here are just a few of the most common myths... debunked:

HSPs are empaths. All empaths are HSPs, but not all HSPs are empaths. You can think of an empath as an individual who meets all the criteria for high sensitivity yet has an additional set of abilities. An empath literally feels other people's emotions, whereas HSPs merely sense them. Empaths are also more vulnerable to negative energy and are more likely to report meaningful spiritual and intuitive experiences.

HSPs are all introverts. While the majority of HSPs are introverts, almost one-third (30%) are actually extroverts!

Don't dismiss the possibility that you are an HSP just because spending time with other people leaves you feeling energized rather than drained. In fact, HSPs can develop a wide circle of friends because they are so empathetic and intellectually stimulating.

HSPs are just shy. HSPs often like to take their time when processing social situations, especially if they are in a noisy environment. To an outsider, their measured approach might suggest that they are shy. This isn't the case. It's more likely that a quiet HSP is just taking a moment or two to reflect on what is happening around them. They might appear slower to speak than others, but this is because they believe in the power of words and, therefore, prefer to think about what they want to say before opening their mouths.

HSPs all have anxiety disorders and/or depression. This simply isn't true. High sensitivity describes a way of thinking and relating to the world, whereas anxiety disorders and depression are mental illnesses. However, HSPs can indeed become anxious and depressed if they don't understand their own needs. They also can experience great suffering if those around them cannot, or will not, understand them. Later in this book, you'll learn how to keep yourself healthy and happy.

HSPs all have Autism Spectrum Disorders (ASD). People with ASD sometimes have problems processing sensory information, and they can become overloaded as a result. In some cases, those with ASD can experience "meltdowns" triggered by excessive sensory input, so it's easy to see why people conflate "highly sensitive" and "autistic."

However, there is a fundamental difference between being an HSP and having an ASD. An ASD is a developmental disorder, not a trait or personality type. To be diagnosed with ASD, an individual must show "persistent deficits in social communication and social interaction across multiple contexts." HSPs do not have problems communicating with other people, and the majority are skilled at social interaction.

HSPs have Attention Deficit Hyperactivity Disorder (ADHD) or Attention Deficit Disorder (ADD), which is why they are so reactive to stimuli. This is simply untrue. ADHD and ADD are psychiatric disorders that usually require treatment, whereas high sensitivity is a natural variation that occurs in one-fifth of the population.

This confusion arises because there are some points of similarity between HSPs and those with ADHD/ADD. Both groups tend to be perfectionists, they both have a well-developed sense of intuition, they both enjoy daydreaming, and they both like to help other people. They also share an appreciation for the arts, frequently feel the need to express themselves creatively, and believe in standing up for the oppressed. As an HSP, you may find that you naturally gravitate toward people with ADD or ADHD.

However, there are a few signs that separate an HSP from someone with ADHD. For the most part, HSPs have the ability to concentrate for prolonged periods of time, which is usually a difficult task for those with ADHD. HSPs are usually better at following the thread of a conversation. However, an overstimulated HSP soon feels overwhelmed, and they might find it hard to complete a task.

To complicate matters further, it's possible to be highly sensitive and be diagnosed with ADHD or ADD at the same time! However, as a general rule, you are likely to be one or the other. Reading this book will help you gain clarity on this point. If you are still unsure, consider consulting a medical professional to obtain a definitive diagnosis.

HSPs are rare. Twenty percent of the population are HSPs. You could argue that this makes them relatively un-usual, but it's hardly a "rare" trait. To put it into perspective, at least one child in every classroom is an HSP, and there might be a few dozen working in a large company! Assuming you know at least five people besides yourself, there's a good chance you know another HSP.

HSPs are more gifted, intelligent, or creative than the average person. This may or may not be true—we don't have enough information yet to know either way! Dr. Elaine Aron, a highly-regarded sensitivity expert, takes the view that HSPs and non-HSPs are probably equally as intelligent and creative.

It's obvious when someone is highly sensitive. If you are an HSP, you probably have chosen to hide this trait from time to time. Most highly sensitive people have taught themselves to conceal their true nature for fear of being judged. For example, if your parents made you feel bad just because you happened to have a sensitive nature, it's almost inevitable that you would get into the habit of pretending to be "normal." As an HSP, you have been blessed with a strong sense of intuition, but don't beat yourself up if another HSP slips past you—over time, sensitive people can become highly accomplished at putting up a façade.

HSPs can be "normal" if they want to change. It's true that an HSP can *act* "normal," but this doesn't mean that they can turn their sensitivity on and off at will. They certainly don't choose to be more sensitive than the rest of the world.

All HSPs prefer a quiet, boring life with little stimulation. Most HSPs value the opportunity to retreat from the hustle and bustle of the world to relax and recharge, particularly if they've had to spend a lot of time in a busy environment. However, this definitely does not mean that they want to stay at home all the time! HSPs tend to be curious about the world around them, so they will go out happily and explore it. Not only that, but extroverted HSPs can thrive in social situations that entail talking to lots of people.

HSPs are weak. Sensitive doesn't mean "weak" or "frail." To survive as an HSP in a world that doesn't understand sensitivity requires strength and determination—in fact, you can't afford to be weak if you're an HSP!

HSPs don't have successful careers. HSPs do have different requirements when it comes to the workplace. For example, as an HSP, you probably dislike jobs that require you to work in chaotic environments for hours at a time. However, as long as you understand and accommodate your needs, there is no reason you can't enjoy a great career.

The key to having a successful career is identifying your strengths and making the most of them. For instance, as a diplomatic person who is reluctant to hurt anyone's feelings, you are in a great position to put forward constructive criticism and potentially controversial new ideas without causing undue offense. This will gain you respect at work. Later in this book, we'll look at how you can pick the perfect career for you.

There's a lot of information to take in when learning about high sensitivity. Fortunately, you don't have to remember all the finer details. Just bear in mind that, as an HSP, you can't help but process the world in a deeper, arguably more meaningful way than the majority of the population. Unfortunately, it's hard to manage your feelings if you don't have the tools to do so! Just because you feel emotions intensely doesn't mean you know how to deal with them. In the next chapter, we'll look at how you can develop your emotional intelligence and why these skills can make your life as an HSP much easier.

CHAPTER 2:

DEALING WITH EMOTIONAL OVERWHELM & BUILDING YOUR EMOTIONAL INTELLIGENCE

You're probably familiar with the concept of IQ—a measure of general intelligence—but have you ever thought about your emotional intelligence (EQ)? In order to understand your personality, skills, and needs, it's important that you understand these concepts in detail.

Those with a high IQ are typically good at working with abstract information, spotting patterns, and generally making sense of information. They tend to perform well at school and are thought of as "smart" and "intelligent."

But what does it mean to be emotionally intelligent? In brief, someone with a high EQ is skilled in recognizing and working with their own emotions and those of other people. For example, they are able to identify when they feel sad and then work out what they can do to feel better. A high EQ is also associated with strong relationships and connections to the broader community.

We can break emotional intelligence into three main components.

Emotional awareness: The ability to hone in on how you feel, understand why you are feeling a particular way, and give each feeling a label. Emotionally intelligent people are not afraid of any emotion. They know that feelings are a natural, normal part of the human experience.

Handling emotions: The ability to process your feelings and those of others in a constructive manner. For instance, someone with a high EQ is able to calm themselves down in a high-pressure situation. They are also able to soothe others when they are hurt and cheer them up when necessary.

Harnessing emotions: The ability to channel your emotions in a useful way, for example in solving problems or expressing yourself creatively. For example, an artist who draws on their personal experiences in creating sculptures is demonstrating their emotional intelligence.

Another way of looking at EQ is to think of it as a collection of skills: self-awareness, social awareness, relationship management, and self-management. The stronger your skills in these areas, the higher your EQ.

WHAT DOES ALL THIS HAVE TO DO WITH HSPs?

You may be highly sensitive, but it doesn't mean that you know how to handle your feelings. HSPs are often good at self-awareness and social awareness, but not so good at self- and relationship management. This means that they can become emotionally overwhelmed, which can take a toll on their mental and physical health. As an HSP, you will always be susceptible to emotional overwhelm, but developing your EQ can help you maintain a healthy emotional equilibrium.

For example, let's say that you are having a busy day at work. As an HSP, you realize that you feel stressed, and you also know that your colleagues feel pressured. Your emotional awareness allows you to pick up on this quickly. Great, but what should you actually do about it?

This is where many HSPs tend to get stuck. They can detect what's going on with themselves and others, but they are clueless when it comes to managing these feelings in a healthy way. An HSP who allows themself to be carried away on a tide of their own emotions or gets bogged down in other people's feelings will soon become miserable.

The good news is that you can learn to develop your EQ and learn skills to improve your self-management and relationships. In the short term, repressing your emotions might lead to temporary relief, but you cannot keep them locked away forever. Unless you learn how to face up to them, they will linger in your body and mind as stress, tension, and illness.

SELF-MANAGEMENT

Here are a few tips to help you learn how to process your feelings when it feels as though they may consume you.

GROUND YOURSELF IN THE MOMENT

Over-analyzing your surroundings and emotions is a recipe for emotional overwhelm. Learning a few basic grounding techniques can keep your stress levels from spiraling out of control. For instance, naming five things you can hear, see, smell, and touch can have a grounding effect.

Some people like to carry a small object or charm in a pocket or purse and hold it in their hand whenever they feel overwhelmed. For instance, you could buy a keyring that carries a positive association for you and squeeze it during stressful times. This can work well but take care not to become too reliant on any one object—if it gets lost, you'll become very stressed! One solution is to buy a packet of small stress balls and put them in your coat pocket, desk drawer, and so on. That way, you will always have one close by, and you won't become too attached to a single item.

You cannot just will your emotions away. Human beings cannot help but react to experiences, whether internal or external. If you tell yourself to "just get over it" or "stop thinking about it," you will only feel worse. Remember that you can't control your reactions, but you can choose how to process your feelings.

The next time you are overwhelmed by emotions, try this exercise as recommended by therapist Dr. Andrea Brandt:

1. Breathe slowly and deeply, in through your nose and then out through your mouth.

2. Cross your arms and hold each of your forearms with the opposite hand. Squeeze. This sensation will help you remain grounded in your body rather than getting caught up in your thoughts and feelings.

3. Recite a mantra or quote that you find to have a calming effect, such as "This too shall pass" or "No feeling is forever."

4. Remind yourself that no feeling is "bad." It's OK to be angry, sad, and stressed. The problem only comes when you can't manage your feelings properly and do or say harmful things to yourself or others.

FOCUS ON THE POSITIVE SIDES OF CHANGE

Do you feel overwhelmed by change? You aren't the only one—both HSPs and non-HSPs can find it tough to accept! The trick is to make a habit of identifying the positives in the situation rather than allowing yourself to dwell on what could go wrong.

The next time you catch yourself panicking about a change, take two minutes to write down any positives you can think of. For instance, if you have to look for a new job because of the risk of redundancy, remind yourself that a new role might offer you a new intellectual challenge. You may be planning to move and are feeling stressed as a result. It might help to write down what you like most about your new home and neighborhood.

Of course, not all change comes with positives. If you have recently lost a loved one or are facing bankruptcy, even the most optimistic individuals would agree that it's hard to find a silver lining. As a general rule, try to take a balanced view of a situation. Unless you are staring utter disaster in the face, there's usually at least one or two blessings or lessons you can take from your personal challenges.

EXPERIMENT WITH NEW WAYS OF EXPRESSING AND HARNESSING YOUR EMOTIONS

Don't allow your emotions to fester. Once you have identified what you are feeling (as an HSP, you are probably good at labeling your emotions), you may need to vent it in some way. Experiment to find out what works for you. Some people find journaling therapeutic, while others channel their feelings through sports, art, singing, or even just punching a cushion or pillow really hard! As long as you aren't hurting yourself or someone else, do whatever is necessary to make yourself feel better.

Feelings are not, in and of themselves, "bad" or something to be feared. They can be a constructive force for change, especially when you harness them in a healthy manner. If you are going through a particularly turbulent time, think of ways you could use the power generated by your emotions to make a positive change. For example, if you have escaped an abusive relationship recently and feel angry and sad on behalf of others in similar situations, you could consider taking on a volunteer role at a local organization serving victims of domestic violence.

USE THE HEALING POWER OF CRYSTALS

Carrying a grounding crystal (such as rose quartz or black tourmaline) in your pocket can help absorb negative energy and reduce your stress levels. They are also excellent meditation aids—hold your favorite stone as you meditate to enjoy greater relaxation. We'll take a closer look at crystals and their special powers later in the book.

MANAGE STRESS BEFORE IT TAKES HOLD

Emotional overwhelm can occur in response to a specific trigger, but sometimes it seems to have no particular cause. This feeling coming "out of nowhere" can be frightening because it feels as though you have no control over your own mind. If you start experiencing emotional overwhelm and don't understand why, take a look at your general stress levels. Background stress can lead to seemingly random emotional outbursts that may come and go without warning.

The solution is to take preventative measures that reduce stress levels and keep your emotions on an even keel. HSPs often respond well to regular meditation practices. You don't need to set aside hours each day—just ten minutes of meditation will offer significant benefits.

To get started with meditation, turn off your phone and any other sources of noise and seat yourself in a comfortable chair or on the floor. Close your eyes and take a few deep breaths. Your goal isn't to empty your mind of all thoughts—doing so is virtually impossible. The purpose of meditation is to help you separate yourself from the mental debris and junk we all have whirling through our heads. It trains you to become a detached observer and teaches you that the majority of thoughts are transient and meaningless.

Focus on your breathing. When your mind drifts, as it inevitably will, do not resist it. Remember, you are acting as an observer. See your thoughts and feelings as clouds or balloons. Let them pass you by. With practice, your thoughts will seem less threatening, which will benefit your everyday life. You'll start to realize that even strong emotions do not last forever.

RELATIONSHIP MANAGEMENT

HSPs often love to form meaningful connections with others, and they typically have a good idea of what those around them are thinking. However, this doesn't necessarily mean that their relationships will run smoothly! From time to time, a sensitive nature can make things challenging.

TRY NOT TO TAKE CRITICISM PERSONALLY

Most HSPs are perfectionists and struggle to take criticism. This presents a dilemma! On one hand, you want to learn from your mistakes and know that you can benefit from other people's advice. You know that receiving constructive criticism can be helpful. At the same time, you can't help but feel personally attacked when someone suggests that you should be doing something differently.

The simplest yet most effective way to deal with criticism is to separate yourself from your work. When someone gives you feedback, remember they are referring to your work, not you as a person. For example, if your boss tells you that you need to rewrite a section of a report, this doesn't mean that you are a failure who can never be trusted to produce good work. Unless you have good reason to suspect otherwise, assume the other person is evaluating only what you have *done,* not who you *are.*

It may seem scary, but receiving feedback and constructive criticism gets easier with practice. Actively seeking out criticism is probably the last thing you want to do, but you'll be surprised how soon you can learn to take another person's advice. If you receive negative feedback, turn it into a list of actionable bullet points. This will give you a sense of control.

For example, if your boss tells you that a report you've written is too long-winded and contains too many statistics, simply writing "Cut sentence length, take out at least a third of the numbers, and use less jargon" gives you a starting point when making revisions.

Another useful tip is to record any positive feedback you receive. You might have noticed that you have the habit of remembering only the negative things people say. Perhaps you discount compliments altogether and worry that your ego will get too big if you believe the nice things your family and friends tell you. Rest assured that this isn't the case. If someone gives you praise, trust that it's for a good reason.

LEARN HOW TO HANDLE CONFLICT IN A CONSTRUCTIVE WAY

Are you conflict-averse? Many HSPs hate the thought of arguing with someone else. Conflict makes the average

HSP feel overwhelmed, and the aftereffects can last for days. Fortunately, reframing conflict and learning a few tricks that nurture your relationships can help you navigate it with grace.

For a start, remember that when someone is angry with you, they are angry because their perceptions have led them to feel a certain way, and their image of you isn't necessarily accurate. Keep this in mind and conflict will start to feel less personal. You can never control someone else's perceptions, but you do have the power to choose what *you* do and say.

The key to handling any argument is first to understand how the other person developed their opinion or arrived at a particular conclusion, and then gently explain why you believe (or know) that this perspective is incorrect. This requires a lot of diplomacy, but luckily for you, HSPs tend to be naturally skilled in this area! Don't attempt to impose your opinion or will at any cost. Tell yourself that you'll get the best results when you try to really understand someone else's point of view instead of trying to "win."

Remind yourself that conflict may be unpleasant, but it will help you develop strong communication skills that will serve you well in the future. For instance, arguing with your partner is no fun, but it may help you at a later date when you need to stand up to a controlling boss. Handling conflicts can also boost your self-esteem—a reminder that you are capable of leaving your comfort zone.

Conflict with those closest to you can be painful, but sometimes it is necessary if the relationship is to move forward. For instance, if your best friend tells you some unpleasant truths about your friendship during an argument, this may hurt, but it allows the two of you to clear the air. Remember that if someone raises their worries directly, it means they probably care a great deal about your relationship.

Finally, you can always ask for some time out from an argument. There is no law that says everyone must resolve their differences in a single conversation! If you need a few minutes to compose yourself or to come to terms with everything that has been said, excuse yourself for a little while. However, don't just leave the room with no explanation, as this will appear dismissive and passive-aggressive.

DRAW UP FIRM BOUNDARIES

Everyone, highly sensitive or not, needs to draw up and maintain healthy boundaries in their relationships. Boundaries let other people know what you will and will not accept from them. For example, in a healthy relationship, both people have boundaries they erect to keep them safe from abuse. Specifically, they will both make it clear that they will not tolerate any form of mistreatment, and anyone who breaks this rule will face consequences.

Whatever your boundaries may be, you need to enforce them. For instance, you might have set a boundary regarding text messages and the time of day at which you will and won't reply. Your rule might be, "I don't read or respond to messages after dinner, which is around 8 p.m." In making this rule, you are setting a boundary—others cannot expect you to read or reply to their messages late in the evening. This kind of boundary keeps you from getting too involved in other people's drama or problems, thereby safeguarding your own emotional wellbeing.

Even if you are clear about your boundaries, there will still be those who might try to overstep them. To continue with the above example, one or two of your friends might still expect a reply and be offended when you stick to your boundaries. The good news is that if you are consistent and assertive (while remaining polite), others will usually come to respect you for standing up for your own needs.

In order to set firm, healthy boundaries, you need to learn how to say "no." In the next chapter, you'll discover how to do precisely that.

CHAPTER 3:

HOW TO SAY "NO" WITHOUT HURTING OTHERS

I n the previous chapter, we talked about the relationship management skills you need to develop to be a happy HSP. One of these skills is so important that it deserves a chapter of its own.

As an HSP, you might have noticed that it's hard for you to say "no" to other people. HSPs tend to value good manners, and they don't like the thought of hurting anyone's feelings. There's nothing wrong with wanting to help out or show some consideration, but always saying "yes," even when you really want to yell "no!" comes at a cost.

Over time, you'll begin to resent those who ask you for favors. You might even turn into a martyr, thinking and saying things like, "Why does everyone else expect me to do everything for them?" and "I never have enough time to myself—my whole life is just one errand after another." You might not stop and realize that if you don't learn how to say "no," you are basically allowing other people to use you as a servant!

When you agree to take on too many projects or chores, you place yourself at risk of emotional overwhelm. Remember, HSPs often become stressed when confronted by a long to-do list. Don't fight against your nature just for the sake of helping someone else. This is particularly true if the other person in question doesn't often go out of their way to lend you a hand. Relationships don't have to be a perfect 50/50 split, but there's no need to wear yourself out helping someone who takes you for granted.

Given that HSPs are likely to be perfectionists, it's perhaps unsurprising that they are usually among the most competent individuals in a workplace. This has obvious advantages—your chances of success increase if you know what you're doing—but there's one notable downside. When everyone knows that you are a capable person who doesn't like to hurt anyone's feelings, they will start to ask you to take on more work. Perhaps you've even had the experience of being assigned leadership or management duties despite the fact you'd rather chew off your own arm than lead a team. "No" is a two-letter word with the power to save your sanity.

Contrary to what you might believe, saying "no" doesn't make you a bad or selfish person. We all need and deserve to have our feelings taken into account when making decisions. Here are a few simple but effective ways you can say "no" and keep your relationships intact.

Make "no" the first word that comes out of your mouth. Assertive people start with a firm "no" when declining a request. Ideally, you'll be able to give a short, simple answer that leaves the other person with no doubt as to where you stand.

For example:
"No, thank you, I can't."
"No, I don't have time today."
"No, that won't be possible."
"No, there isn't room in my schedule for that."

If someone continues to push you, they are in the wrong—you are not.

Just because saying "no" feels unpleasant, doesn't mean that it isn't the right response. Suppose someone asks you on a date. If you happen to be in a relationship, simply saying, "No, thank you, I'm not single," will work fine. But what if you just don't find the other person attractive and don't want to hurt their feelings? You could lie and say that you're already seeing someone, which might be a good idea if the person asking you is a stranger. However, if the two of you move in the same social circles, it won't be too long before they realize that you are single.

In this situation, you need to remind yourself that saying "no" is the only humane option. The alternative is to do something that will make both of you unhappy further down the line. In the case of declining a date, it's far better to endure a few moments of awkwardness than to date someone for several weeks (or even months) before working up the courage to tell them that you were not interested in the first place.

Remember too that a reasonable person will be able to tolerate a "no thanks." Your only obligation is to remain civil, thank them for asking, and decline with grace. If they continue to ask despite your refusal or start to harass you, they are the one with a problem!

Do not apologize. Apologies are only appropriate when you have done something wrong. Politely turning down a request isn't morally wrong or even rude, so there's no reason to say you're sorry. If the asker continues to put you under pressure, they should be apologizing, not you. Instead of saying "sorry," you can soften a refusal with phrases like "No, thank you. I would like to but…," "No, that won't be possible because…," and "No, thank you. It's too bad, but I can't do it because…"

Keep your body language positive. When saying "no," make a conscious effort to relax your shoulders, make eye contact with the other person, and smile politely. You don't have to be aggressive, just assertive. It may sound silly, but it can help to practice declining a request in front of the mirror!

Do not make excuses. There's no need to devise an elaborate explanation or excuse for why you cannot do something. Not only is a refusal a complete answer in its own right, but elaborate cover stories can come back to haunt you. Even if you pride yourself on having an excellent memory, there's a chance that you'll forget exactly what was said, which could result in embarrassment later on.

If the other person doesn't realize you are just making an excuse, they might try to "help" you out, and the conversation may soon move into awkward territory. For instance, if you tell someone that you don't want to see a musical with them on Friday night because you can't get a babysitter, they might respond by telling you that they can give you the number of a great babysitter or suggest that the two of you go out the following week instead. You will then be forced to give another excuse!

Use the broken record technique. Have you ever encountered someone who doesn't seem able to take a hint and keeps repeating the same old question over and over again? There are a couple of reasons this happens. Some people are just plain pushy, persistent, and rude. Others might assume that you'll inevitably say "yes" if they keep asking the same question over and over again, particularly if you've always said "yes" in the past.

Fortunately, the broken record technique is an effective way to shut down these people. To use the broken record technique, simply repeat your answer again in exactly the same tone of voice. Maintain the same facial expression, use the same words, and look them straight in the eye every time you respond. After a few rounds, they will begin to feel silly and self-conscious.

If you know someone who wouldn't mind helping, pass on their name. Under no circumstance should you try to pawn someone off onto a third party just because you aren't brave enough to say "no." However, on some occasions, the best thing to do is recommend that the other person approach someone else who might be able to help. For example, if a colleague asks you for help with a project and you already have far too much work to do, it's fine to recommend that they approach someone else who you know has both the time to offer assistance and would be happy to do so.

Compliment the person who asked you for a favor.
Some people react badly when they hear "no" because they assume that the other person is rejecting them as an individual, along with their request. If you are dealing with someone like this, it's a good idea to offer them a compliment if possible. For example, "You're such a hard worker, I know you'll make the project a success one way or the other" would be a suitable compliment to give someone when telling them that you won't be helping them with their assignment.

If someone is harassing you, spell out the consequences. Unfortunately, some people believe that they are entitled to your help and support whether or not you want to give it to them. Occasionally, you will meet someone who becomes angry or even threatening when you turn down their request. It may be tempting to give in for the sake of preserving the peace, but this won't work out well in the long run—they will assume that they can use intimidation tactics to get their way.

The best approach is to defend your boundary by informing them of the consequences they will face if they continue to push the issue. For example, you could say, "I have already told you that my answer is 'no.' If you continue to ask me inappropriate questions in the workplace, I will report it to an HR representative."

DOES YOUR SELF-IMAGE HINGE ON SAYING YES?

You've probably heard time and time again that you are a "nice" person who can always be relied upon. It's a wonderful reputation to have, but has it come to be a central part of your identity? Take a moment to really think about your answer, even if it makes you feel uncomfortable, because it may help explain why you are so reluctant to turn people down.

No one is totally exempt from caring about what everyone else thinks of them, including HSPs. If you take pride in being the person who never lets anyone down and always lends a hand, you might be reluctant to say "no" because it means losing a part of your identity. It may help to remind yourself that you don't have to say "yes" at every opportunity to be a good person. Think of the nicest people you know. I bet that some of them (if not all of them) have mastered the art of saying "no."

As an HSP, you probably find a lot of satisfaction in helping others, but this doesn't mean you have to extend help at every opportunity. Saying "no, thank you" may not come naturally, but it's a skill you can learn. These little words will not only free up your schedule, allowing you to focus on the people and activities that matter most to you, but it will also help you shore up your boundaries and prevent others from taking advantage of you. As you will learn in the next chapter, an unprepared HSP is vulnerable to exploitative individuals, so it's a good idea to remain on guard for them.

CHAPTER 4:

HOW TO AVOID FALLING IN LOVE TOO QUICKLY, FILTER OUT UNHEALTHY PARTNERS, AND ENJOY A GREAT RELATIONSHIP

A ccording to sensitivity experts, HSPs are prone to falling in love quickly in a dramatic fashion, which can be an intoxicating, exhilarating experience. Unfortunately, intense love affairs often crash and burn. This can be painful for anyone, but HSPs are particularly vulnerable to heartbreak. It's important to learn how to safeguard your heart and take a relationship at a steady pace, even if you are tempted to dive straight in at the deep end!

HSPs are not irrational, but they are often driven by their feelings when they meet someone they find attractive. If you are an HSP, you are in danger of pursuing someone who isn't necessarily right for you just because they make you feel good. Another danger comes from settling. Have you ever felt so lonely and misunderstood that you'd be willing to date (or even marry) the first half-decent person who crossed your path? It's OK—many of us have been there! HSPs love emotional intimacy. Unfortunately, if you are too desperate to find someone, your judgment and intuition might take a back seat.

DON'T ASSUME THAT ONLY ONE PERSON CAN MAKE YOU HAPPY

As an HSP, you can't control your feelings, but you can gently challenge some of the more unrealistic ideas you have about love and romance. Idealism is a charming trait, and it inspires some HSPs to change the world. Unfortunately, an HSP in love can fall into the trap of casting someone in the role of "The One" and come to believe that only that one other person can make them content.

It's a romantic idea, but it simply isn't true! If you think about it, most people have several relationships before they settle down with a long-term partner. When you are caught up in a whirlwind of daydreams and hormones, it's easy to lose perspective. Remember the EQ skills you learned earlier in this book? Here's the perfect opportunity to put them into practice! They will help you remain grounded and will also provide you with the tools you need to form a healthy bond.

WATCH OUT FOR PEOPLE WITH SERIOUS PROBLEMS

In theory, you might think that an HSP would be drawn to another sensitive person because they both have similar wants and needs in a relationship. In reality, it's a little more complex than that! If you've been dating for a while, you may have noticed a strange pattern emerging. It's likely that some of the people who find you attractive seem to require hours of love, support, and even re-parenting. If you suspect that others see you as an emotion sponge or even as a counselor, you're probably right.

It's not your fault. As an HSP, your natural empathy makes you highly attractive. That's the good news. The bad news is that some people, whether they have malicious intentions or not, are drawn to you in the hope that you can fix them. Being the helpful person that you are, reluctant to risk hurting anyone's feelings, you've probably found yourself taking on the role of armchair psychologist at some point. If you allow this arrangement to continue, you may never be free. You become too emotionally invested in the other person and can't bear to think of them struggling alone.

So, what should you do? Prevention is better than cure. The most important thing you can do is to realize that other people's problems aren't yours to solve, and they certainly shouldn't form the basis of a romantic relationship. If you are dating someone and discover that they have a serious problem or character flaw, think very carefully before continuing.

Ask yourself this: Do I really want to become entangled with someone who appears to have significant psychological and emotional problems? Do I really want to take on the role of someone's unpaid counselor or aide? Do not confuse "tormented" or "in pain" with "intriguing" or "challenging." Base your choice of partner on whether you share values and interests not on whether you can play the role of helper!

How to Spot a Toxic Person

Narcissistic individuals and energy vampires target HSPs. They tend to assume that because HSPs love helping others, they will give them the endless supply of attention and validation they so desperately crave. Don't fall for it. They will treat you well at first, then discard or abuse you when they start taking you for granted. Learn the danger signs that signal a narcissist or energy vampire and avoid dating them at all costs.

Here are the key warning signs that suggest someone may be a narcissist:

1. They like to talk about themselves all the time. At the start of your relationship, they might ask you a lot of questions, but this isn't because they are actually interested in your life—they simply want to hook you in.

2. They sincerely believe that they are "the best" at everything.

3. They believe they deserve everything life has to offer, even if they don't put in much work.

4. They prefer to hang out with people they perceive as "important" or famous. Status is more important to them than meaningful connections.

5. They often leave you feeling drained, confused, or pessimistic after a day or night together. Even if you haven't had an argument and everything seems

OK on the surface, they still manage to bring your mood down.

6. They will happily cast themselves in the role of a victim to get what they want.

Next are a few indicators that someone is an energy vampire. Note that not all energy vampires are narcissists, but all narcissists are energy vampires!

1. They see everything through a lens of negativity.

2. They will happily gossip about other people behind their backs, which means they are probably gossiping about you too.

3. They don't congratulate you when you succeed. They may even belittle your achievements.

4. They talk about themselves all the time and expect you to listen to them for hours.

5. They don't respect your boundaries.

6. They are jealous of others who have the material possessions or type of relationship they want for themselves.

7. They use passive-aggressive behaviors such as giving you the silent treatment when you don't do as they ask.

If you've been blindsided by someone's good looks and charm, it's not always easy to spot these signs. You may be so keen to see someone for what you want them to be, rather than what they are, that you enter a state of denial. Sometimes, you have to learn these lessons the hard way.

Don't beat yourself up. HSPs and non-HSPs alike sometimes chase people who are toxic or simply not right for them. Just don't let yourself make the same mistake twice. If a close friend suggests that you are involved with someone who isn't right for you, try not to get defensive. Listen to what they have to say, and then decide for yourself whether their concerns are justified.

TRUST YOUR INTUITION

Your intuition is one of your greatest gifts as an HSP. Trust it! Your intuition may not always tell you what you want to hear, but it's there for a reason. For instance, suppose you are dating someone who calls regularly, plans great dates, and compliments you all the time, and yet your inner voice tells you that something isn't quite right.

If your intuition is telling you that something's wrong, it's time to back off a little, slow down, and watch for signs indicating that your partner isn't quite everything they appear. Sometimes a partner may be acting strangely because they are unsure how to conduct themselves in a relationship, or because they are insecure and afraid of doing something "wrong." It's OK to give them a little while to reveal their true selves. In fact, the wisest people make a point of taking their relationships at a slow pace. If the two of you are right for one another, then what's the rush anyway?

SHOULD YOU DATE ANOTHER HSP?

On the surface, finding another HSP may seem to be a good idea. After all, you'll be able to understand one another's struggles and personality types, right? Well, yes—but two HSPs won't automatically make for a happy couple.

The typical HSP-HSP pairing runs into problems because both partners are aware, sometimes to a painful extent, of the other person's moods. Each will pick up on their partner's emotional disturbances, which can be exhausting. Because HSPs tend to be people-pleasers, they might both worry about satisfying their partner in all areas of the relationship—sometimes to an excessive degree. When something goes wrong in the relationship, they both tend to assume the blame, which keeps them locked in misery.

On the other hand, if both HSPs are self-aware and continually working on their own self-development, their relationship can be very fulfilling. As long as both partners are willing to openly express their emotions, talk through troublesome issues, air their grievances in a constructive manner, and take responsibility for their own emotions, they can look forward to many years of happiness. However, both parties must be sufficiently invested in both the relationship and their personal growth.

MAKE PLANS THAT DON'T REVOLVE AROUND YOUR LOVE LIFE

In Chapter 2, you learned that HSPs often have plenty of self-awareness but lack skills in self-management. This means that you may be painfully aware that you are in love or have a raging crush on someone but aren't sure what to do about it.

Although it's impossible to stop thinking about the other person when you're in love, continuing to build your own life and future will help you maintain a healthy distance and move on if it turns out they aren't right for you. If you allow yourself to focus on the other person to the detriment of your personal development, you'll have so much energy and emotion invested in the relationship that you'll be reluctant to let go. On the other hand, if you have a full and active life, it will be easier to detach from an unhealthy relationship that isn't going anywhere.

Be sure to keep in touch with your friends. Make it a policy never to look to just one other person for emotional nourishment, because you will be in a vulnerable position if they leave you. To some extent, it's normal to spend less time with your friends in the early days of a romantic relationship, but you should never abandon your friends entirely!

SPEAK UP IN THE EARLY DAYS OF THE RELATIONSHIP

As an HSP, you are tuned in to other people's emotions—sometimes to a painful degree. Your empathetic nature and warm heart draw in people who have problems and need someone to listen. Have you ever been told that you are "so easy to talk to" or "such a good listener"? This is a common experience among HSPs. Although it's great to lend emotional support to others, you can end up taking on the role of an emotional sponge or unpaid therapist unless you learn how to balance your own needs with your desire to support others.

Don't let your natural desire to earn someone's love take priority over your own comfort and needs. Learn how to say "no" and stand your ground! In the early stages of a relationship, you may be all too happy to put your partner first always. Unfortunately, this sets a dangerous precedent. It sends your partner a clear signal—"I'm here to make my own needs secondary to yours, and I'm happy to act as your personal servant!"

This attitude rarely results in a healthy relationship. Your partner will assume that you have low self-esteem, that you don't have a mind of your own, or that you are unusually submissive. There's a risk that any relationship that develops will be based on an unequal power dynamic, whereby one person (your partner) drives the relationship and the other person (you) plays the role of servant and passenger. You might wake up months or even years later wondering where your life has gone!

STOP EXPECTING PERFECTION IN YOUR RELATIONSHIPS

As one of nature's perfectionists, the harsh reality of relationships can seem like too much for you to handle. For example, most couples fight from time to time, and you should expect a degree of conflict between yourself and your partner. In fact, if the two of you never fight, one or both of you are likely repressing your true needs and opinions. That isn't healthy!

If you are serious about finding and keeping a long-term relationship, you must accept that there is no such thing as the perfect partner, and there is no such thing as the perfect relationship. This doesn't mean you have to settle for the first person you find, just that you need to be prepared to compromise in some situations.

You also need to be open to constructive criticism and feedback and be willing to speak up in order to get your needs met. It may not be romantic, but no one—not even HSPs—can read minds! Don't fall back on unrealistic romantic notions such as believing that true love entails knowing precisely what the other person thinks.

WHY HSPs FIND IT PARTICULARLY HARD TO DEAL WITH A BREAK-UP

It's fair to say that few people feel good when their relationship comes to an end. Even if we have known for a long time that our partner isn't the one for us, it's still painful. Unfortunately, as an HSP, you are even more vulnerable to the difficult feelings that accompany heartbreak. Whereas most people will feel sad and empty for a while following a breakup, HSPs often feel as though their world is literally collapsing around them.

If you are recovering from a broken relationship, remember that it's normal for HSPs to require a longer healing period than the majority of the population. It's harder for you to let go of the feelings and memories associated with your former partner, along with the hopes and dreams you had for the future. This is true even if you were the one who ended it! Imaginative HSPs can spend hours agonizing over what they could or should have done differently, or even picturing what their partner might be doing without them.

What's the best way to deal with a breakup as an HSP? You may have read books or articles advocating that you go "No Contact" with a former partner once the relationship has ended. To put it simply, going "No Contact" means that you do not see, call, or talk to your ex. Neither should you stalk their social media profile or ask mutual friends how they are doing.

In some cases, it isn't possible to go completely "No Contact." However, it's probably the best thing to do if you're an HSP. Why? Because it gives you the best chance of moving on. In the short term, it will feel like agony; but in the long term, you will be much better off. It keeps you from feeding your own obsession and encourages you to look toward the future. "No Contact" also keeps you from running back into your ex's arms only to be hurt again. Trust that they are an ex for a reason. If the two of you were right for one another, the relationship would not have ended. Remember too that there is more than one person in the world who can make you happy.

The period following a breakup is also the perfect time to practice your self-management skills. Specifically, think of ways you can channel and come to terms with your feelings. Don't just sit on them and hope that they go away! Talk to a trusted friend, seek out a therapist, write about your feelings, take up a new hobby—do whatever it takes, as long as it doesn't hurt your physical or mental health.

Finding the right romantic relationship can be tough for an HSP, but there's no need to feel disheartened. A non-HSP can develop relationship skills and learn from their mistakes, and you can do the same! Relationships can be challenging for everyone, regardless of where they fall on the sensitivity scale. Yes, you might experience the pain of heartbreak more acutely, but you also have the capacity for deep love and affection.

CHAPTER 5:

HOW TO ELIMINATE NEGATIVE ENERGY

As an HSP, you are much more vulnerable than others to the effects of negative energy, whether it comes from other people or the environment. Everyone reacts differently when exposed to it, but common symptoms include fatigue, feelings of nausea, headaches, muscle aches, and a motivation deficit. Negative energy can make you physically and mentally ill, so you must learn how to eliminate it! In this chapter, you'll learn several techniques that will protect you from its effects.

WORK ON CULTIVATING A POSITIVE ATTITUDE

There is quite enough negative energy in the world already, so why add to it? The Law of Attraction states that your personal vibration and energy level determines who and what comes into your life. In practice, this means that if you decide to look upon the universe with an open mind and a loving heart, you will attract positive people and energy.

In a world full of negative media that encourages us to think about what is going wrong rather than all the positive things that are going on all around us, this is easier said than done. You need to be proactive in changing your attitude. Start by cutting down the amount of time you spend watching and reading the news. Yes, it's good to stay informed when it comes to current affairs, but the majority of news media is full of sensational stories that are produced to "entertain" rather than inform.

Choose to be optimistic. Some of us are naturally more inclined to see the sunny side of any situation, but anyone can learn to be more positive. Watch your own thoughts. What do you think when you open your eyes in the morning? Do you look forward to the day ahead, or do you just want to roll over and go back to sleep?

Every morning, make a point of asking yourself what you are looking forward to in the coming hours. Just before you go to sleep each night, give thanks for at least ten things you enjoyed that day. They can be big things, but the little things count too. For example, be sure to give thanks if you enjoyed a fantastic cup of coffee with your breakfast or found a free parking space the moment you arrived at the mall that afternoon.

Try keeping a positivity journal. Every day, write down a few things for which you are grateful, together with any quotes that inspire you or compliments you have received from others. You can also record your hopes and dreams for the future. If you are working toward a particular goal, you can monitor your progress.

HARNESS THE POWER OF EARTH, WATER, OR FIRE

Earth, water, and fire can all be used to absorb and transform negative energy. Begin by meditating for a few minutes and clarifying your intentions—to discharge the negative energy that has been building within you. Imagine it moving as a single, dark mass down your arms and into your hands. To discharge it, place your hands in water (ideally, free-flowing water found in a natural environment, but a shower will also work), directly onto the ground outside, or toward a naked flame.

As you do so, picture the negative energy flowing out of your body, through your palms and into the element. Don't worry about spreading negative energy—each element has an infinite capacity to reshape it and deliver it back to the universe as a positive force.

BRING NATURE INDOORS

You've probably noticed that it's easier to feel positive when spending time outside. Trees, grass, flowers, and running water all filter negative energy and promote a sense of wellbeing. However, it isn't always possible to simply take a walk when you're stressed or upset.

Luckily, you can bring nature indoors! Start by placing at least one plant in each room. This will foster a positive atmosphere that will make it easier to shake off negative energy. Some varieties are particularly beneficial.

BAMBOO

A favorite of Feng Shui practitioners, bamboo is considered a potent symbol of luck and health. It represents the wood element, which improves general vitality and promotes positive energy. Traditionally, a bamboo display is made up of an odd number of stalks, as this is thought to bring more luck. Keep it in a bowl of shallow water out of direct sunlight.

SAGE

Sage is popular for its ability to remove negative energy from the environment. As a bonus, it also has a pleasant smell, making it a good choice for kitchens and conservatories. Sage plants are prone to drying out so ensure that their soil is kept moist.

PEACE LILIES

A peace lily purifies the air around it, removing harmful gases and toxins such as carbon monoxide and benzene. It also facilitates the smooth flow of positive energy. Peace lilies look beautiful and are relatively low maintenance. They do not require much light, so they can be placed in windowless rooms.

ORCHIDS

Feng Shui experts believe that orchids act as lightning rods for positive energy, promoting great emotional and spiritual health. They are well known for their charming scent, which elevates the mood of all who smell it. To keep your orchid healthy, simply water it when the soil becomes dry.

HOLY BASIL

Used in Ayurvedic medicine as a means of cleansing the air of toxic energy, holy basil will give your home an instant energy boost. It can also be used to purify water, which can then be sprinkled in every room in your house to improve the flow of positive energy. To enjoy the maximum benefit of this plant, place it in an east, north, or northeastern part of your house or garden.

OTHER WAYS TO CLEAR YOUR HOME OF NEGATIVE ENERGY

A messy home encourages negative energy to fester, whereas a clean, tidy space permits the flow of positive energy. Keep a clutter-free home when possible and get rid of objects you no longer use. This is particularly important if certain objects hold bad memories for you, as their negative energy can directly act on your body and mind. Repair broken objects, as they are another source of bad energy according to Feng Shui philosophy.

Make sure your home gets fresh air and sunlight. Draw back all the curtains and leave them open as long as possible. Open the windows for at least a few minutes every day. Fresh air purifies negative energy and helps you stay upbeat and optimistic.

Smudging is a quick and easy way to rid yourself and your home of negative energy. All you need to do is light a bundle of sage, blow it out, and then walk around your house while swirling the bundle in a counter-clockwise direction. Start in the hallway and work your way through every room.

Consider adding a water feature to your home. For instance, you could invest in a tabletop water fountain. The sound of running water is immensely soothing. Our bodies are primarily composed of water, and our water molecules are permanently in a state of vibration. If you raise the rate at which your water molecules vibrate, you can eliminate negative energy.

When you are close to an external source of water, its vibration will affect the water inside your body. The purer the external source, the more positive your internal energy will become. A moving water feature will therefore reduce the negative energy in your body, restoring a sense of tranquility and peace. If you do not like or cannot afford a moving water fountain, simply keeping a large transparent bowl of clean water in plain sight is an alternative option.

Finally, you can use saffron to eliminate negative energy from your surroundings. It emits a pungent scent that is said to repel negative energy and malevolent spirits. You can mix it in with water, leave it to steep for a few minutes, then sprinkle the infusion around your home to purify the environment.

PLAY BINAURAL BEATS & PURE TONES

Music changes the atmosphere of a home or workspace, and it can help clear negative energy fast. There are many free recordings of binaural beats and pure tones available online that will raise your body's vibration, stimulate your chakras, and help wash away a toxic aura. Some people find that listening to natural sounds, such as recordings of waves crashing against a shore, helps them restore their energy levels.

LAUGH

Laughter is one of the fastest ways to clear negative energy and make yourself feel better. When you've had a tough day, find something that makes you laugh, even if it's just a five-minute video on YouTube. Laughter triggers the release of endorphins in your brain, which lowers stress levels and can even act as natural painkillers.

Why not put together your own laughter library so you always have some funny material on hand whenever you need it? For instance, you could keep a shelf filled on your bookcase for light-hearted reads or compile a playlist of comedy recordings on your phone. If you like cartoons, keep a few stuck to your fridge or stick them on a pinboard near your desk.

CLAP & SING

The simple act of clapping your hands is enough to break up negative energy. Singing also promotes the flow of positive energy through your body and is a quick way to boost your mood. You might feel self-conscious at first, but after a couple of minutes, you'll be glad you tried it! For maximum effect, pair it with high-frequency music.

TRANSFORM YOUR NEGATIVE ENERGY INTO PRODUCTIVE ACTION

When a problem or person is dragging you down, challenge yourself to list at least three potential courses of action you can take to remedy the situation. For example, if you hate your job and arrive home each evening feeling burdened by negative energy, could you come up with a plan of action that would either help you find a new position or at least enhance your current working environment?

If it's a person who keeps draining your energy, what could you do to improve your relationship with them? Sometimes it's as simple as making a few adjustments to your routine to minimize the amount of contact you have with them, such as choosing to take lunchtime a bit earlier or later to avoid running into a toxic colleague.

Let me be clear—not every situation is so easy to solve, and sometimes the best we can do is use tools that clear negative energy while making the most of a suboptimal job or relationship. However, many people get so caught up in their own negativity that it doesn't occur to them to sit down, carefully weigh their options, and channel their energy into devising a solution that will make them feel better. Empower yourself by taking a realistic look at your life and thinking about what you can do to change it.

OFFER OTHERS A HELPING HAND

When you help someone else, you spread positive energy and make the world a brighter place. Not only will the person you are helping feel grateful, but your self-esteem will also skyrocket. Showing someone else kindness is instant proof that you really can make a difference—you are here for a reason!

SPEND TIME WITH ANIMALS & PETS

Research has shown that people with pets tend to live longer, have stronger immune systems, enjoy better cardiovascular health, and report lower levels of stress. Therapy animals are often brought into residential homes for elderly people and those with disabilities. There is no doubt that pets are a powerful source of healing.

Playing with a cat or dog will quickly improve your mood and help eliminate any negative energy you've accumulated throughout the day. Their life force ("chi") will raise your energy. Animals live in the present; they do not waste time worrying about the past or fearing the future. We have much to learn from them. Watching wild animals in a park or in the woods can also be relaxing.

PROTECTING YOURSELF FROM NEGATIVE ENERGY - SHIELDING

As the saying goes, an ounce of prevention is worth a pound of cure. As an HSP, mastering the art of shielding yourself against negative energy will save you a lot of trouble. Shielding protects you from emotional contagion, meaning that you won't automatically pick up on everyone else's emotions. Just as a solid physical shield protects a soldier from enemy blows, an energy shield will deflect aggression, hopelessness, and other negative emotions that other people may knowingly or unintentionally send your way.

You can shield yourself in three simple steps.

1. Imagine a wall or barrier separating your body from everyone and everything around you. This barrier can take the form of a ring of light, a gate, or a glowing shield. Some people find it easier to imagine that they are wrapped in a white light. It doesn't matter what form your shield takes as long as it helps you feel safe.

2. Remind yourself that you can choose what passes through the shield. Picture yourself receiving good energy and positivity in the form of smiles, compliments, and sincere words of praise. Allow yourself to imagine feeling uplifting, secure, and content.

3. Visualize your shield keeping out bad energy. Imagine negative energy simply bouncing off it and away from everyone in the room. Remind yourself that you get to choose what can and can't penetrate your barrier.

If you know in advance that you will be exposing yourself to negative energy—for example, if you are attending a meeting with tense, angry, or pessimistic people—meditate privately for a few minutes beforehand. Take this time to breathe deeply, ground yourself in the present, and engage in creative visualization.

Resist the urge to reflect someone's negative energy back in their direction. This is difficult to do because when someone else engages in negative behavior, it's tempting to give them a taste of their own medicine. For example, if someone makes a sarcastic remark, you may feel inclined to give a cutting answer. However, this approach helps nobody. At best, it maintains the negative energy in the environment. At worst, it culminates in open conflict that hurts both parties.

You have many options when it comes to eliminating negative energy from yourself and your surroundings. As an HSP, learning how to handle negative energy is a skill you must learn for the sake of your physical and emotional wellbeing. You don't need to remember every tip and technique—just experiment to find two or three that work for you and be ready to use them the moment you suspect your energy balance has been disturbed.

CHAPTER 6:

DEALING WITH DEPRESSION AS AN HSP

High sensitivity isn't a mental illness, but some HSPs are at an increased risk of depression and anxiety compared with the general population. Fortunately, a few lifestyle adjustments, coupled with self-awareness, can safeguard your mental health. In the following chapters, you'll learn why some HSPs are more prone to mental illness than others, and what you can do if you notice the signs of depression or anxiety.

HSPs and Depression

Depression is a serious mental illness that affects around 20% of the population at some stage in their lives. Depression isn't simply a bad mood—its main symptoms include feelings of hopelessness, lack of energy, weight changes, inappropriate guilt, and decreased motivation. If you think you might be depressed, it's important to make an appointment with your doctor.

Psychologists don't know for sure what causes depression, but most Western doctors believe that it is caused by an imbalance of chemicals within the brain. People with depression often experience symptoms following a stressful time in their lives, but it can also start for no apparent reason. This can also apply to HSPs. In other words, you don't need a reason to be depressed.

However, although each case is different, HSPs appear to be especially vulnerable in certain situations. Let's start by looking at the most common reasons HSPs become depressed.

OVERSTIMULATION, HELPLESSNESS, & DEPRESSION

When an HSP is chronically overstimulated, they may come to feel helpless, and helplessness can be a precursor to depression. Psychologists have long known that if someone feels as though they have no control over their own lives, they are prone to feelings of despair and depression. For example, suppose an HSP starts a new office job, and within a few days, they realize that the environment is far too noisy for them; in fact, they keep getting headaches and even feeling nauseated at the thought of going into work.

What could the HSP do in this situation? They could quit their job, but that probably isn't a good idea unless they have another lined up. Asking their boss and coworkers for reasonable accommodations, such as permission to work with headphones on when possible, probably would be a better idea.

However, let's say that their boss isn't particularly sympathetic and just tells the HSP to get on with their work. In this kind of situation, an HSP is forced to stay in an environment that causes them a lot of distress. Knowing that there is nothing they can do, they will likely become depressed. To make matters worse, the more depressed they feel, the less energy they will have to look for solutions such as finding alternative employment.

FEELING LOST OR "DIFFERENT" CAN TRIGGER DEPRESSION

Another reason an HSP may become depressed is that they don't understand why they feel so different from everyone around them. They may become lonely and come to the conclusion that they will never find someone who truly understands them. It can be hard to strike a balance between pursuing relationships on one hand and seeking solitude on the other. It can take years to find the right match, and the wait can take a toll on an HSP's morale.

PAYING ATTENTION TO THE STATE OF THE WORLD CAN TRIGGER DEPRESSION

An HSP can become despondent easily about the state of the world. There's no denying the sheer amount of suffering experienced by animals and humans alike. Even non-HSPs sometimes despair when they contemplate poverty, disease, and so forth. Over time, an HSP may feel almost grief-stricken by the thought that they can't do anything to fix the world's problems.

To make matters worse, they may wonder why those around them don't seem too concerned. They may come to believe that they "care too much" and that they need to "toughen up." Some HSPs have decided, whether consciously or not, that it's best to try to ignore the bad things that happen in the world. This might help them feel less distressed in the short term, but emotional suppression isn't healthy. In some cases, it can lead to an inability to feel any emotions at all, which increases a person's vulnerability to depression.

PERFECTIONISM

HSPs tend to be deep thinkers, and they often hold themselves to high standards. On the plus side, this can make them very successful. However, there is a dark side to perfectionism. If you are a perfectionist, any mistake—even if it's relatively minor—will be a blow to your sense of identity. Of course, maintaining high standards over a long period of time is mentally and physically draining, which increases vulnerability to depression and burnout. We'll look at how to deal with excessive perfectionism later in this book.

DEPRESSION & BURNOUT IN HSPS

Burnout is a state of total depletion in which an individual experiences mental and physical exhaustion. Although it can result in a crisis (sometimes known as a "breakdown"), it's more likely to take the form of a slow decline. Someone in a state of burnout becomes numb to the world around them. They literally cannot take on new tasks and see no point in carrying on. In extreme cases, burned-out people require several months of rehabilitation before they recover fully.

Unfortunately, HSPs are more prone to burnout than non-HSPs. In the workplace, an HSP is usually forced to deal with busy environments, high workloads, office politics, and the pressure to conform. This is why many HSPs prefer to be self-employed—they get to manage their own environment and workload and can take a step back as soon as they identify the earliest signs of burnout. In the next chapter, you'll learn how to cope with stress at work.

YOUR EARLY ENVIRONMENT & DEPRESSION

For both HSPs and non-HSPs, being raised in an unhealthy environment can increase someone's vulnerability to depression in later life. For instance, we know that those who were abused as children are at a significantly higher risk of mental illness as adults.

HSPs are especially susceptible to depression if they grew up in an unsupportive, invalidating environment. A sensitive child living in a dysfunctional household will be bombarded by other people's negative emotions, and this experience leaves long-lasting psychological wounds. On the other hand, an HSP who was accepted and loved as a child is somewhat protected against depression. However, they can still suffer if they are stuck in a seemingly hopeless situation or feel alienated from the rest of society.

DO YOU SPEND TIME WITH NEGATIVE OR DEPRESSED PEOPLE?

As an HSP, you feel both your own emotions and those of others keenly. On the plus side, this makes you a wonderful and supportive friend. Unfortunately, your tendency to absorb other people's feelings puts you at risk of emotional contagion. While you can't "catch" depression, you can certainly feel low or even despondent if you spend too much time with someone you know or suspect to be depressed. It takes a strong HSP to maintain a healthy relationship with someone fighting depression, but you can help them while protecting yourself. Check in with yourself and set some firm boundaries.

For example, if you notice that someone has fallen into the habit of calling you several times a week to talk about their problems, you need to check in with yourself and take an inventory of how these interactions make you feel. If you realize that your conversations with this person leave you feeling down for several hours afterward, it's time to let them know that you need to either cut back on the number of conversations you have with them or talk about more positive (or just neutral) topics instead.

How to Handle Depression as an HSP

As you can see, there are many reasons you might become depressed as an HSP. So, how can you safeguard your mental health? It depends on the reason you feel low, but here are some tips.

Accept that you are different

Acknowledging your status as an HSP is helpful and healing. Thanks to the numerous online communities that have sprung up on the internet, you no longer have to feel alone.

There are plenty of supportive blogs and websites that will help you make the most of your special trait. When you take healthy pride in being an HSP and connect with others, you will no longer feel alienated. Given that 20% of the population is an HSP, you might also be able to find another HSP and support one another. Look out for those at your workplace or school that might be highly sensitive. Try to strike up a friendly conversation. You might make a new friend.

GET ENOUGH TIME ALONE

We've already established that HSPs require a lot of space. If you lead a busy lifestyle, it's easy to fill your schedule up to the extent that you don't have time for yourself. All too often, HSPs suddenly realize that their lives are too full and they have little opportunity to retreat from the outside world.

Schedule time for yourself in the same way you would plan any other activity, and honor that commitment. Yes, your work and relationships are important, but spending time alone is essential for your mental health. Think in advance of what you would like to do during these periods. Just sitting in a relaxing bath with a good book might be all you need to feel better after a tough day.

WORK ON LEADING A HEALTHIER LIFESTYLE

Most of us know that our bodies and minds are interlinked. The saying "healthy mind, healthy body" is a cliché for a reason. Cutting down on alcohol, reducing your intake of processed foods, getting more exercise, sticking to a regular sleep schedule, and making time to relax for at least a few minutes every day can do wonders for your mental health.

FOCUS ON FORMING & MAINTAINING POSITIVE RELATIONSHIPS

If spending time with depressing people is hurting your mental health, what's the antidote? Spending time with uplifting people, of course! You are readily influenced by other people's moods, so use it to your advantage. Even if you are highly introverted, try to socialize with those who lift you up at least a couple of times each month. When you have no choice but to interact with negative people, use your shielding skills to protect yourself from emotional harm.

LEARN HOW TO CHALLENGE NEGATIVE THOUGHTS

Depression is a complex illness with many possible causes and manifestations, but most professionals believe that it is sustained by habitual negative thinking. For example, many depressed people assume that they are boring, un-appealing, and have little to offer the world. They may regularly think to themselves, "No one would ever want to talk to me," "I'm utterly useless," or "I'm not worth listening to."

You can see how this type of negative thinking keeps depression going. It's like having a bully following you around all day, whispering (or shouting) nasty things in your ear. Even the most naturally optimistic person would struggle to feel happy if they had to listen to unrelenting negativity all day.

Fortunately, you can learn to identify and challenge your negative thoughts. This exercise will help you.

1. Identify your negative thought and write it down.

2. Note how the thought makes you feel. For example, if you think, "I am ugly," you may feel worthless or upset as a result.

3. Ask yourself the following questions and think carefully about the answers.

    - Do I have any evidence that contradicts the negative thought?
    - What would I say to someone else in the same situation?
    - Is this a helpful way to think?
    - Can I think of a more balanced thought that won't make me feel as bad?

This process won't be easy at first but with enough practice, you'll be able to do it anywhere. It doesn't matter whether you believe your new balanced thoughts at first—a depressed brain requires serious retraining. You may wish to check out books on Cognitive Behavioral Therapy (CBT) to learn more techniques to challenge your negative thoughts. If you feel overwhelmed by the prospect of doing this work alone, consider seeing a therapist.

CONSULT A THERAPIST OR COACH WHO CAN HELP YOU MAKE CHANGES IN YOUR LIFE

As you know, feelings of helplessness can result in depression. To tackle the root cause, you need to identify the areas of your life that need fixing and devise a plan of action that will help you take back control. Learning how to handle your emotions will help you deal with emotional overwhelm and depression in the short term, but the only viable long-term solution is to take a long, hard look at your lifestyle and situation and make whatever adjustments are necessary for your mental health.

Unfortunately, it can be hard to do this alone, particularly if your motivation has disappeared and you aren't even sure how to begin fixing your problems. This is where a good therapist or coach can help you. They can provide an objective view of your situation, equip you with the skills you need to solve your own problems, and provide emotional support as you make changes. They can also help you work through maladaptive thought patterns and take a more positive approach to life.

You can ask a medical practitioner to refer you to a psychotherapist or you can search for a qualified professional by visiting the official websites of counseling training and regulatory bodies. For example, in the U.S., you can find a therapist at counseling.org, the website of the American Counseling Association.

Earlier in this chapter, you learned that some HSPs may be prone to depression if they grew up in a disturbed or chaotic home. If this applies to you, you might also need to process difficult childhood experiences and work through past trauma with the help of your therapist.

DON'T FORGET TO CLEANSE YOURSELF OF NEGATIVE ENERGY

In Chapter 5, we looked at how and why you should be proactive in eliminating negative energy from your home and life. When you sense that your mood is about to take a downward turn, consciously choose to eliminate negative energy from your body and space. Set aside an afternoon to clean and tidy your home. Ask a friend or relative for help if you are low on energy and motivation.

When you are depressed, basic self-care can be a chore. Grounding, smudging, meditation, and other helpful techniques that you would usually enjoy can feel impossible. Do not push yourself too hard. Challenge yourself to do one thing every day that helps remove toxic energy from your life. For instance, you could try 10 minutes of meditation practice one day and promise yourself to cleanse your home of negative energy by smudging it the next.

CONSIDER COMPLEMENTARY TREATMENT OPTIONS

If you feel depressed, it's important to see your regular doctor. He or she can carry out tests to ensure that your symptoms are not caused by another condition, such as thyroid problems. If you receive a diagnosis of depression, you might be advised to take antidepressants.

Medication works for some people, but some HSPs find conventional treatments unpleasant and ineffective.

Although antidepressants can cause side effects in anyone regardless of their sensitivity levels, HSPs are particularly vulnerable to nausea, skin rashes, digestive complaints, and other problems that can arise when taking these drugs. Of course, they are sometimes necessary to help an HSP through a crisis. If you have been prescribed a drug, you should never stop taking it without consulting a medical professional.

Complementary therapies that involve energy work can also be useful for HSPs who struggle with depression. For example, you could consider seeking out a Reiki practitioner. Reiki is a form of energy healing based on the theory that a trained therapist can facilitate the movement of energy from their hands to a patient's body merely by using the power of touch. According to Reiki practitioners, we all have "life force energy" that powers our bodies and minds. If these energy levels drop, the result is fatigue and susceptibility to illness. During a Reiki session, a therapist restores the body's life force energy, which leads to feelings of relaxation, positivity, and peace. You remain fully clothed throughout the treatment, and there is no pain or discomfort involved.

You Can Do It!

Depression is a frightening illness, but you don't have to suffer alone. Although there is still a stigma surrounding mental illness, people are more willing to talk about these issues than ever before. Being an HSP does not mean you are doomed to live a life ruled by your emotions, and neither does it mean that you are destined to get depression. In fact, if you take charge of your self-development and learn how to work with your feelings, you will be safeguarding yourself against mental illness.

CHAPTER 7:

DEALING WITH ANXIETY AS AN HSP

An HSP who lacks insight into their special trait might assume that they are just a jittery, anxious person destined to live a life of worry. Fortunately, it doesn't have to be this way. As you've made your way through this book, you will have come to appreciate why an HSP can easily feel overwhelmed and anxious. In fact, it's almost inevitable—being caught in a tsunami of emotions and energy fields naturally has a significant impact on a person's wellbeing. The good news is that when you develop self-awareness and self-management skills, you won't have to suffer from chronic anxiety.

THE DIFFERENCE BETWEEN HIGH SENSITIVITY & ANXIETY

To the untrained eye, high sensitivity and anxiety disorders appear similar. In fact, many people use the words "sensitive" and "anxious" interchangeably. For example, someone with a phobia of small spaces will have panic attacks whenever they have to spend time in a large crowd. Their symptoms—feeling overwhelmed, shaky, jittery, and physically unwell—are the same as those reported by HSPs when they are highly stimulated.

Although not all people with anxiety disorders are HSPs and not all HSPs have anxiety disorders, there is a link between anxiety and sensitivity. HSPs tend to have particularly sensitive startle reflexes, which make them more prone to heightened emotional arousal. An individual's reflexes are determined by their genetics, which partially explains why HSPs typically report that sensitivity seems to run in their family.

Just to make matters worse, the average HSP has a vivid imagination that can fuel their anxieties even further. This is a downside of creativity! They are all too capable of imagining worst-case scenarios, which further feeds into their anxiety or panic. For example, if they feel especially shaken in a noisy environment, they may start to wonder whether they are having a heart attack and even begin to worry about how their family or friends will deal with the news of their death! This may sound melodramatic or ridiculous to a non-HSP, but the distress people with this trait feel is real.

The key difference, of course, is that non-HSPs with anxiety disorders can approach their anxiety as a mental illness that can be eliminated entirely with the right treatment. On the other hand, an HSP will never fully eliminate their sensitivity and susceptibility to anxiety and panic. If you are a particularly anxious HSP, aim to get your tendency to worry under control rather than to overcome it completely. You can help yourself cope with high levels of intense stimuli, but you will always have a lower stress threshold than a non-HSP.

Tips for Anxious HSPs

Ride the wave of anxiety – Don't try to fight it

The best way to combat anxious thoughts and panic attacks is to accept what is happening and ride them out. Resisting your feelings will only make them worse. Think of it like this—if someone tells you not to think about a polar bear, what happens? You think about a polar bear, of course! The same principle applies here.

It's impossible to shut down a panic attack once your nervous system has sprung into action. When you begin to panic, your body releases adrenalin that triggers your fight-or-flight response. At this point, you have a choice to either try to reason your body out of its symptoms or choose to accept what is happening and wait it out.

Therapist Linda Walter, who specializes in working with anxious people, recommends the R.I.D.E. technique. It's a simple acronym that can help you handle even the roughest of panic attacks!

Recognize: Acknowledge that you are having a panic attack.

Involve: Choose to engage with your surroundings. Use grounding and breathing exercises to keep yourself rooted in the present.

Distract: This step is self-explanatory. All you need to do is find something that holds your attention, even if it's just for a few moments.

End: Trust that even the scariest of panic attacks usually pass within a few minutes, and almost all attacks end within 30 minutes.

It may not feel like it, but anxiety can't kill you. You have the strength to make it through to the other side!

A mantra is another useful tool. Come up with a phrase or saying in advance and repeat it to yourself during difficult times. For instance, you could tell yourself, "This will pass," or "I just need to wait." Write it on a card and keep it in your purse or wallet so you have it on hand. You could even make it your phone wallpaper!

MASTER BREATHING EXERCISES

Breathing exercises can make you feel better during times of high anxiety. Practice slow, deep breathing when you are calm until it becomes second nature. You will then be able to use this technique when anxiety strikes. To calm yourself down, begin by inhaling through your nose. Picture the air filling your lungs. Hold your breath while counting to three. Purse your lips and exhale slowly. As you breathe out, make a conscious effort to relax your body. Pay particular attention to your neck, shoulders, stomach, and jaw.

A variation of this exercise is the "Calming Counts" technique. Find a comfortable place if possible and sit down. Begin by inhaling slowly and deeply. As you exhale, tell yourself to relax. Next, take ten normal breaths. Shut your eyes and keep them closed as you count down, either in your head or out loud. You can also ask someone else to count for you if you feel very worried and unable to concentrate. As you do this exercise, make a conscious effort to relax the muscles in your body.

WATCH FOR PATTERNS

Some people find that their feelings of worry and panic appear to come and go at random, but there are usually some underlying triggers. Pay close attention to the events preceding your periods of anxiety and panic. You can then make a plan of action. For example, if you seem to get anxious around a particular person, you will need to work on your energy shielding, use your boundary-setting skills, or learn how to resolve disagreements. If a particular environment makes you feel tense and panicky, use the techniques outlined in this book to cleanse it of negative energy.

Remember that if you are generally stressed and anxious, it won't take much to tip you over the edge into a panic attack or a state of emotional overwhelm. To thrive as an HSP, you will benefit from getting into healthy habits, such as regular meditation and energy work, that will help you manage stress.

FIND A SYMPATHETIC MENTAL HEALTH PROFESSIONAL

If your feelings of anxiety are causing you a lot of distress, or you are having problems functioning at home or work, you should consider seeking professional help. However, it's important that you choose a doctor or therapist who appreciates that some people are simply more sensitive than others, and therefore have different needs. You may need to take anti-anxiety medication if your symptoms are severe, but it's usually more effective to take a long-term approach and learn to manage your feelings.

For example, a non-HSP who has developed an anxiety disorder following a difficult period in their life can reasonably expect to make a full recovery and return to their usual low levels of anxiety, but an HSP should not be encouraged to change their personality just to fit in with society's idea of "normal."

When attending an initial consultation, ask whether they are accustomed to working with HSPs. If they aren't familiar with the term, say something like, "You see a lot of people, so you know that some people are just naturally more sensitive. I'm in that camp!" You could even bring some literature on high sensitivity with you. A caring, open-minded health professional should be willing to listen. If not, find someone else who is more on your wavelength.

UNDERSTAND YOUR PAST

In the same way that past experiences can lay the foundations for depression, they can also make you more prone to worry and anxiety. For example, if you were bullied as a child or teenager, you might be reluctant to trust others and find yourself panicking in social situations. Sometimes, simply becoming aware of these patterns is enough to help you feel better. However, working with a therapist is beneficial if your worries are deep-seated.

MAKE CHANGES TO YOUR DIET

No one eats a perfectly healthy diet all the time, but it's worth making a few changes because your diet can make a huge difference in how you feel. Don't aim for perfection because you'll only make yourself more anxious!

Cut down on sugar. Too much sugar can lead to difficulty concentrating, visual disturbances, and fatigue. Sugar highs lead to dramatic crashes, which can accompany the physical and psychological symptoms associated with anxiety, such as shaking and feelings of panic. Although sugar does not directly cause panic attacks, its effects can make you feel as though you might have one, and your worries can bring on the real thing.

Skip the fruit juice. Do you prefer to drink juice rather than eat whole fruit? If so, it might be time to cut back. When you eat a piece of fruit, your body digests it slowly. The sugar hits your bloodstream at a modest rate. However, when you drink juice, your blood sugar will suddenly spike before crashing soon after, which can worsen or trigger anxiety.

Pass on the alcohol. Alcohol can help you feel calm, but the effects are only temporary. You risk developing an alcohol dependency if you get into the habit of using it to help you relax. You will also disrupt your blood sugar and sleep schedule after just a couple of glasses, which won't help you feel better!

Reduce your caffeine intake. Be careful not to drink too much caffeine. Stick to one or two caffeinated drinks per day and avoid it after 2 p.m. You may find that even a little bit of caffeine is too much and choose to cut it out of your diet altogether. Remember, HSPs often have sensitive bodies that react strongly to stimulants. Chocolate contains caffeine (along with processed sugar), so restrict your intake to a small amount once or twice a week.

Experiment with a gluten-free diet. Many people with gluten intolerance and celiac disease report feelings of anxiety. Research carried out with celiac patients suggests that their anxiety levels drop once they have cut out gluten for a year, and some doctors believe that people with non-celiac gluten sensitivity are also prone to feelings of anxiety when they ingest gluten. Dr. Rodney Ford, who has a special interest in the effects of gluten on the body, believes that it might trigger or overstimulate the nervous system, giving rise to feelings of worry and panic. Given that HSPs have highly reactive nervous systems, it makes sense that they might be more sensitive to gluten than the average individual.

There is relatively little work in this area to date, but anecdotal evidence suggests that eliminating gluten may be effective in controlling anxiety in some individuals. If your anxiety hasn't responded to self-help, therapy, or medication, you could try a gluten-free diet. However, it's best to work with a doctor or dietitian if you want to try this kind of eating plan as it can result in malnutrition if not carried out under proper supervision.

CARRY CRYSTALS

Blue lace agate, rose quartz, and black tourmaline are just three crystals commonly recommended by healers treating people with anxiety. They carry positive vibrational energy that has a soothing effect on the nervous system. To get the most benefit from a crystal, wear it as a piece of jewelry so that it is in constant contact with your skin. If this isn't possible, you can carry a crystal in your pocket. When you meditate, hold a crystal in the palm of your hand to cleanse yourself of stress and tension.

When choosing a crystal, allow your intuition to guide you. If you feel that a particular stone is right for you, that's the one you should buy! To cleanse them of negative energy, leave them in strong sunlight or moonlight for a few hours.

Anxiety is a common problem for HSPs. Fortunately, there are many steps you can take to help regulate your mood and control your worries. The best approach is to combine a healthy lifestyle with self-awareness, energy work, and specific techniques you can use to help you deal with panic attacks and waves of anxiety.

CHAPTER 8:

PICKING A CAREER & THRIVING AT WORK

The right working environment and career can be very fulfilling for HSPs. However, as a sensitive person, you need to find a path that will allow you to develop your skills and share them with the world without putting you at risk of burnout. In this chapter, we'll look at the kind of jobs best suited for HSPs. You'll also learn about the most common problems HSPs run into at work and how to deal with them.

WHY YOUR CAREER NEEDS TO BE REWARDING

As deep thinkers, HSPs are not happy unless they work in a job that lets them make a meaningful impact in the world. HSPs don't necessarily need or want a big salary or impressive title, but they won't last long in a career that makes them think, "Why am I doing this?" Some people are able to see their jobs as a means to an end, but an HSP needs intellectual stimulation and a sense of purpose.

WHAT CAREERS ARE BEST FOR AN HSP?

As an HSP, you are creative, empathetic, conscientious, and able to tune in to other peoples' thoughts and feelings. This puts you at an advantage in jobs that require original thinking, building relationships with other people, and taking care of details.

JOBS THAT MAY SUIT YOU AS AN HSP

Every HSP is different and must forge their own career path. However, here are some ideas you might like to consider:

WORK THAT INVOLVES CARING FOR OTHERS

Teaching: As an HSP, your patience could make you a wonderful teacher. Students appreciate teachers who take the time to explain difficult concepts from multiple angles and give them plenty of time to fully digest and understand a new idea. Teaching can also be a good way to express your creativity; coming up with new classroom activities and games can be lots of fun.

Social work: Social workers hold families and communities together. The best social workers are nonjudgmental and dedicated to improving their clients' lives. Many HSPs have a strong desire to nurture and care for vulnerable people, another asset that helps them succeed in this field.

Medicine, Nursing, & Midwifery: Like social work, these professions require a commitment to supporting and helping people in difficult circumstances, which is fulfilling for many HSPs.

Psychotherapy/Counseling: Your natural empathy, intuition, and desire to help other people with their problems is a great foundation for a career in psychotherapy. Counseling is a challenging profession for an HSP because it's easy to pick up on your clients' feelings. Fortunately, a good training program will teach you how to draw firm boundaries between your personal life and professional practice.

JOBS THAT LET YOU USE YOUR KNOWLEDGE TO MAKE THE WORLD A BETTER PLACE

Policymaking: If you like the idea of helping people lead healthier, happier lives, but don't want to deal with clients or service users face to face, public policymaking could be an alternative career path.

Law: Working with disadvantaged groups or doing pro bono work could provide you with the right balance of detail-oriented work and an opportunity to help people in need.

Researcher or academic in the social sciences: Many HSPs are fascinated by human behavior and have keen observation skills. If you are also comfortable with numbers and have strong written communication skills, a research career in these fields could be a great fit.

JOBS THAT INVOLVE CARING FOR ANIMALS

If working in a caring profession appeals to you and you have a special affinity for animals, you could consider working as a vet, veterinary nurse, animal trainer, groomer, pet sitter, shelter worker, or welfare officer.

JOBS IN THE CHARITY SECTOR

Any job that involves working for a charity can give you a sense of purpose because you know that your efforts are contributing to a worthy cause. For example, working in the IT department of a charitable organization typically requires very little contact with others, but the role is important for the running of the organization.

CREATIVE PROFESSIONS

Artist/Designer: There are dozens of potential avenues you could explore, including movie set designing, fine art, and illustration. If you don't think you have much artistic skill, you could enter a profession that lets you spend a lot of time around art and creative people, such as gallery curation or art historian.

Actor: Great actors step into the shoes of their characters; they draw on their empathy and imagination to tell a story. Most HSPs are introverts, so it may seem strange to consider a career in acting. However, you don't need to be the center of attention to succeed in the profession, and many introverts have rich imaginations.

Photographer/Videographer: Most photographers and videographers work alone or in small teams. These careers are attractive for creative introverts because they can "hide" on the other side of a lens but still express themselves via their work.

OTHER IDEAS

Spiritual teacher or minister: Many HSPs value spirituality. If you belong to a religion or spiritual tradition and enjoy mentoring people, consider a career that allows you to support people as they embark on their spiritual journeys.

Yoga teacher: You probably understand, better than most people, the value of taking time to relax and be mindful. Yoga can be a physical exercise, a spiritual discipline, or both. If you have a passion for yoga, teaching it could be a good career choice.

Human resources (HR): As someone who is finely attuned to human behavior and has the diplomatic skills required to resolve difficult situations, you could be well-suited to a career in HR.

A leadership position in a values-driven company: You might have been told that leaders need to be extroverted, but this simply isn't true. There are several different styles of leadership, and in the right environment, quiet, thoughtful, sensitive leaders can flourish. For example, some companies prize a style called "servant leadership," in which a leader takes care of their team's needs before their own.

Librarian: If you like helping people but prefer to work in a low-key environment, you may enjoy a career in library science, especially if you have a natural love of order.

Writer: Most writing positions involve a lot of lone work, and an increasing number of writing jobs are fully remote. If you are an introvert who likes to have complete control over their environment, writing could be perfect, especially if you get to write about topics close to your heart.

WHY SELF-EMPLOYMENT CAN BE A GOOD CHOICE FOR HSPs

Many HSPs find it hard to "fit in" at work and get passed over for promotions or other opportunities even if they work hard and want to climb the ladder. If this sounds familiar, setting up your own business may be more fulfilling. You'll get to choose your working conditions, set your own hours, and employ people whose personalities and working habits complement your own. For example, if you want to run a wedding photography business but feel overwhelmed at the prospect of marketing your services at large trade shows, you could hire an extroverted assistant to set up and oversee your booth.

However, there are downsides to running your own business. Even if you work hard and have a sound business model, self-employment can be riskier than working for someone else. It's normal for self-employed people to find themselves in "feast or famine" cycles, and this can be stressful. If you like the idea of working for yourself but aren't sure whether you can cope with these pressures, try starting a side business while you're still employed.

THE TWO QUESTIONS EVERY HSP SHOULD ASK AT A JOB INTERVIEW

Choosing the right field is important, but you also need to find a business that offers an HSP-friendly environment. The best way to gauge whether a position will be a good fit for you is to pay close attention during a job interview and ask the right questions when you get the opportunity.

Remember, a job interview should be a two-way conversation. Here are two questions that will give you some valuable information:

Question 1: "How would you describe the company culture?"

If the interviewer tells you that the culture is fast-paced and everyone is expected to meet tight deadlines, ask yourself whether you could cope with working in a high-stress environment. Listen to your gut. Most HSPs need to work in a place that allows them to express their emotions and take some time out when they feel overwhelmed. If your prospective employer seems to have a "suck it up" attitude, you may have to hide your feelings, which isn't easy for a sensitive person.

Question 2: "Can I take a tour of the office/workspace?"

Most interviewers will offer to show you around during the interview. If they don't, ask them to show you where you'll be working.

Look at the surroundings. Is there anything that makes you uncomfortable or overstimulated, such as bright lights or strong aromas? As an HSP, things that would only be a minor inconvenience to others can be a big problem for you. Make eye contact and say "Hi" to a couple of employees. Do they appear to be enjoying their work? Are they friendly?

COMMON PROBLEMS AT WORK, & HOW TO HANDLE THEM

PROBLEM #1: COMPASSION FATIGUE

People working in the caring professions, whether they work with animals or humans, need to protect themselves against compassion fatigue and burnout. Signs of compassion fatigue include:

- Irritability
- Difficulty sleeping
- Low job satisfaction
- Weight loss
- Tearfulness
- Feeling alienated or "cut off" from everyone
- Emotional and physical exhaustion
- Feelings of resentment towards the people or animals you care for

- Self-doubt; you might feel as though you "aren't good enough" for your job
- Trouble switching off at the end of a working day; you might start feeling worried about your patients or clients outside of normal working hours

You're at high risk of compassion fatigue if you regularly work with people who are traumatized, grieving, or receiving treatment for a mental illness. Compassion fatigue doesn't make you a bad or uncaring person, even if it feels that way.

TREATING COMPASSION FATIGUE

Here's how to look after yourself if you have signs of compassion fatigue:

Take a break: If you have some leftover vacation time, take it. A few days away from work can help you feel a lot better. Otherwise, take some sick leave. You might feel guilty for taking time away, but consider this: If you're burned out, you aren't performing to the best of your ability. For the sake of your colleagues, clients, or patients, taking a break is the most responsible thing you can do.

Reconnect with your personal values: When you are bogged down in the everyday tasks of work, it's easy to lose sight of why you chose to enter the profession. When things are going well, what do you gain from your job? How does it help you realize your potential as a human being? Reflect on the moments that have made your career fulfilling.

Tell someone how you are feeling: Reach out to a friend, relative, or trusted colleague. Talking through your problems can help you gain perspective. Burnout is surprisingly common; you might discover that they have had a similar experience.

See your doctor: If you are so stressed, anxious, or depressed that you can no longer function normally, make an appointment as soon as possible. You may benefit from therapy, medication, or a combination of the two. There is no shame in seeking help in a crisis.

PREVENTING COMPASSION FATIGUE

Build a good relationship with a mentor: Find someone you can confide in about the problems you face at work. In most cases, this will be a manager or senior colleague. If you work independently in a caring profession—for instance, as a self-employed counselor—you may need to seek out and pay for ongoing supervision. As soon as you notice the signs of compassion fatigue, seek your mentor's advice. They'll be able to guide you on self-care and help you decide when it's time to take a break.

Be proactive: Identify the parts of your job that cause you the most stress and start thinking about how you can cope with them in the future. Perhaps you already have some coping skills, but maybe they aren't working as well as they used to, or you could benefit from some training and support at work.

For example, in the early days of your career, venting with your coworker about a difficult day might have been enough to make you feel better. However, if you've since been promoted or taken on more responsibility, your everyday stress levels may be much higher, and stress management training could help you.

Remain self-aware: Every day, pause a few times to tune into your emotional and mental state. For example, when you wake up in the morning, how do you feel? If the answer is "tense" or "nervous," don't brush it off—ask yourself what is making you feel this way, and why. You may need to make some changes to your working day; perhaps you need to delegate more of your work or schedule in some regular breaks.

Seek personal therapy: If you feel guilty about your compassion fatigue and feel depressed, it may be time to get some personal therapy. This is especially important if you have, or have had, a mental illness that makes you vulnerable to stress.

Get into a healthy routine to protect your body and mind: When you're tired and eating a poor diet, your emotional health will suffer. Refer back to the previous chapter for some tips.

Be prepared to make a bigger change: If your job is stressful and you can't find a coping mechanism that works for you, it may be time to consider looking for a new position.

PROBLEM #2: FINDING MEANING IN YOUR WORK

It's important for an HSP to do meaningful work, but it's not always possible to find a job that fulfills you. For example, you might be stuck in a job because there aren't many opportunities nearby, or perhaps you are working a less than ideal job to put yourself through college.

Here are a few strategies you can try:

Keep learning: If you get a chance to pick up a new skill at work, take the opportunity. Learning engages your brain, and mastering a task, even if it doesn't align with your broader career aspirations, can bring a sense of fulfillment. Teaching someone else can also be satisfying, so if you have the time and the skills, volunteer to mentor or train a new starter.

Be a changemaker: Initiate positive change at work— something that benefits both the organization and its employees. For example, if your employer doesn't have a recycling policy in place, could you set up a "Green Committee"? Or, if there's no disability or diversity awareness training, would it be possible to talk to your HR department about setting up a workshop?

Keep your resume up to date: Every time you gain some new experience at work, refresh your resume. Write down notes on what you did, any additional responsibilities you took on, and how it benefitted your employer. By the time you leave your job, you'll have a record of everything you've achieved. It will make writing your next job application letter easier too because you'll have a useful summary.

Look for meaningful friendships: Even the most boring of jobs can be bearable if you make a good friend. Be open to making connections with coworkers. Try not to make assumptions or be swayed by first impressions. Until proven otherwise, treat everyone as though they have good intentions.

Look at the bigger picture: If you're in a job because you are still training or studying for the career you really want, think about the kind of work you'll be able to do when you've earned your degree or certification. Or remind yourself that there is more to you and your life than your work.

Set aside a portion of your wages for a cause you care about: Allocate a percentage of your salary for a charity of your choice. This doesn't have to be very much; if you can only afford $10 per month, it's still enough to make a difference.

Problem #3: Everyday stress

We've already covered several stress management strategies in this book, including mindfulness and exercise. Most of them can be adapted for work. For example, taking a brisk walk at lunchtime or doing a breathing exercise at your desk will help you feel calmer. Here are a few extra tips for handling everyday pressures:

Set up a positive space: If you're allowed to decorate your workspace, add a few touches that make you feel at home. Get a potted plant for your desk. HSPs often find solace in the natural world, and adding some greenery to your workspace can give you a mental boost. Put up a few photos of landscapes, animals, or anything else that gives you a sense of peace. If you'd like to befriend your coworkers, put a dish of candy on your desk and tell everyone that they can help themselves. You'll have a chance to make conversation every time they stop by.

Get clarity: A major source of workplace stress is ambiguity. If you are a perfectionist who wants to do a good job—like most HSPs—uncertainty will make you anxious. Make a point of asking your supervisor or another coworker if you need guidance. Some employers offer regular performance reviews and feedback sessions, but others expect their workers to somehow know what's expected of them. If your boss falls into this camp, you need to get comfortable with asking questions. Suggest that the two of you hold a quick meeting or check-in by phone every week to make sure everything is on track. If they put up any resistance, tell them that you'd rather risk looking ignorant and asking a few unnecessary questions than do a bad job. Make it clear that it's in their interest to hold regular reviews.

Get comfortable: You can't expect to feel relaxed if your chair, desk, and other equipment aren't fit for use. For example, a chair that doesn't support your lower back can cause chronic pain and discomfort, driving up your stress levels and decreasing your productivity. As an HSP, you are more in tune with your body than others, so it's particularly important to look after yourself at work.

If you need any reasonable adjustments, ask your manager. It's in their interest to keep their employees comfortable. Depending on the laws in your area, they may also have a legal obligation to set up an ergonomic workspace.

Don't forget to take care of your eyes. When working at a computer, stop every 20 minutes to gaze 20 feet into the distance for 20 seconds. The "20-20-20" rule prevents eyestrain and headaches. Every hour, get up, walk around, and give your eyes a complete break.

Use a transition ritual: Transition rituals help you leave work behind when you leave at the end of the day. For example, you could put together a playlist of soothing music and listen to it on the way home from work. Give your sensitive nervous system a chance to calm down when you get in the door. If you live with other people, tell them that you need some time alone every day.

PROBLEM #4: GIVING NEGATIVE FEEDBACK

When you have to give feedback, it can be tempting to hold back because you don't want to hurt the other person's feelings. However, if you want them to improve, you must be prepared to point out their areas of weakness.

Open the meeting by telling your colleague that you want to help them make the most of their talents and excel in their role. Explain that you know how hard it can be to get negative feedback and that you'll do all you can to help.

Use examples to back up your points. This keeps the conversation focused on facts rather than feelings. For instance, if you are giving feedback to a junior colleague who often misses deadlines, have a list of projects and dates handy. Give practical, step-by-step instructions or suggestions rather than vague demands. For example, "Have you considered learning new time management techniques?" is more helpful than "It would be great if you could finish your work more quickly."

You may not enjoy these conversations, but your natural empathy gives you a big advantage. Your coworker will realize that you aren't out to bully them and will lower their defenses. They may even share things with you that they'd never bring up with other, less empathetic people. For instance, if their work performance has been suffering because they have been depressed or their relationship is breaking down, they may decide you are a "safe" person to tell.

If you aren't sure what the other person needs, ask them—they might have already given the problem some thought. In some cases, a quick online course or seminar might be all that's needed to bring their skills up to speed. Bear in mind that some people find it hard to respond under pressure. Tell them that it's OK if they need a couple of days to think it over. Encourage them to send you an email if they think a training course or other resource would help.

End the meeting on a positive note. Emphasize that you believe in them and their ability to improve. Tell them that you are looking forward to working with them to grow their skills, and thank them for their contribution to the workplace. Schedule a follow-up meeting to review their progress.

PROBLEM #5: OFFICE GOSSIP

Some people see workplace gossip as harmless, or even as a fun way to bond with coworkers. As an HSP, you probably don't agree. You probably can't understand why spreading rumors about people or saying hurtful things behind their backs is ever acceptable. Here are some tips for dealing with gossip:

Lead by example. Model good behavior. Stay respectful of everyone, whether or not they are in the room. If a coworker tries to bring you into a toxic conversation about someone else, quickly excuse yourself from the situation. If doing so wouldn't get you into trouble, make your views clear. Saying "I don't feel comfortable gossiping, let's talk about something else" or "I don't like to spread rumors about people, can we change the topic?" is an effective way to shut the conversation down.

Give people something positive to talk about. Coworkers sometimes gossip because they are bored. If there's not much going on at work, why not take the initiative and create a positive distraction? Something as simple as a few board games in the break room can be enough to lighten the atmosphere and bring people together.

Let rumors fizzle out. If you are the target of a silly rumor, the simplest solution is to ignore it. Most of the time, your coworkers will move onto another piece of gossip within a few days. Of course, if it could have serious repercussions for your career or reputation, talk to your manager or HR department.

If you have a problem with someone, address it with them directly. Don't complain about a coworker behind their back. It won't solve the issue, and they will probably learn that you've been griping about them.

If you are in a management position, be direct and transparent with your team. Try to stop any rumors about big changes at work, such as redundancies or mergers, before they begin by giving your team as much information as possible. If you don't have all the answers, be honest.

Follow your natural inclinations as an HSP—be truthful, balanced, and compassionate.

If you see or hear a member of your team gossiping, discreetly pull them aside and explain that their behavior isn't appropriate. Remind them that if they have a problem or question at work, it would be more productive to consult you instead of gossiping.

CHAPTER 9:

PARENTING AS AN HSP

HSPs make excellent parents. They are loving, support-ive, and help their children grow into emotionally intelligent adults. They are conscientious and want to improve. Their children feel able to express their feelings and are likely to develop good self-esteem.

However, becoming a mom or dad comes with a set of challenges that test HSPs. Becoming a parent is a huge change for everyone, but highly sensitive parents can have a particularly tough time.

In this chapter, we'll look at some of the most common problems HSP parents face and how to overcome them. You'll also learn about the signs of postpartum depression. Finally, you'll learn how to support a highly sensitive child.

LOOKING AFTER A YOUNG CHILD CAN MAKE YOU FEEL "TOUCHED OUT"

Babies and toddlers require a lot of touch, which can be overwhelming if you're an HSP. Being annoyed or even re-sentful of your child can make you feel guilty; most people assume that if you really love your baby, you'll be happy to let them cling to you all the time.

Another problem is that if you are touched out, your relationship can suffer. At the end of a long day spent caring for your child, the last thing you might want to do is cuddle with your partner. This can lead to resentment on both sides of the relationship—you want a break from being touched, whereas they feel neglected.

Although this is a generalization that certainly doesn't apply to everyone, mothers are more prone to feeling "touched out" than fathers because they tend to do more of the early childcare, particularly if they are breastfeeding.

Communication is key. Don't let your partner have to guess what's wrong. Tell them! Set aside some time for a conversation; wait until your child is in bed and pick a time when neither of you is tired. Acknowledge that your physical relationship has changed and ask them how they feel about it. Listen carefully and without judgment.

Seeing a couples' therapist is a smart move if your relationship is starting to break down, but sometimes the solution can be as simple as splitting childcare more equally to give both parents time to rest and recharge.

ANXIETY IS PART OF PARENTING, BUT MAY FEEL UNBEARABLE FOR HSPs

It's normal to worry about your child or your parenting skills, particularly if you're a first-time mom or dad. But HSPs are especially vulnerable to this kind of anxiety. They are so attuned to their child's emotions that they take on their baby's distress and are quick to blame themselves if they can't work out what their baby needs.

Going to parenting classes, reading books, and sharing your worries with your partner can help you feel better. If you have any friends or relatives with kids, they may be willing to pass on useful tips. You'll soon discover that no one is born knowing how to care for a baby. Childcare is a skill, and, like any skill, you'll get better at it the more you practice.

Teach yourself the basics of child psychology. You'll find many books and articles on the topic online and in your local library. Ask your pediatrician for recommendations. It's hard to watch your toddler have a meltdown or your teen slamming their bedroom door in a rage. As an HSP, you may absorb their emotions and feel a strong sense of guilt. Understanding how children develop emotional intelligence and social skills can help you gain a sense of perspective. Even the most caring, patient parent has to contend with their child's outbursts. Your child's tantrums don't make you a "bad mom" or "bad dad."

If you have a vivid imagination, it's easy to conjure up worst-case scenarios such as your child falling ill or being kidnapped at the grocery store. These thoughts can be very distressing, and there is a fine line between taking reasonable precautions and giving into irrational thoughts. If your worries are so intense that they are making everyday life difficult, talk to your doctor or healthcare provider. They will be able to reassure you and offer practical safety tips if necessary.

Talk kindly to yourself when your inner critic starts criticizing your parenting skills. Don't try to convince yourself that everything is fine, but do try to take a more balanced view of the situation. For example, if you catch yourself thinking, "Why does my daughter always have meltdowns at the grocery store? I'm a terrible mother!" try telling yourself, "My daughter does have tantrums sometimes when we go shopping. It's very embarrassing and difficult to deal with, but it's totally normal. I do the best I can to cope when it happens, and that's good enough."

These days, it seems like the world is a scary place. We're surrounded by media that feeds us a steady stream of bad news. It's easy to conclude that your children are in constant danger. It might help to know that, in many ways, children are safer than ever. For example, child abductions, school violence, and accident fatalities have dropped in recent years. Children today also have more access to resources and educational opportunities than any previous generation. So, while it's completely normal to worry, try to keep things in perspective.

BEING RESPONSIBLE FOR CHILDREN CUTS INTO YOUR "ME TIME"

From the moment your baby is born, they become the center of your world, requiring attention 24 hours a day. As a new parent, grabbing ten minutes for a shower is a luxury some days, and "me time" becomes a distant memory.

As an HSP, you need space to rest and recharge. Becoming a parent doesn't change that. Needing and taking regular breaks doesn't mean you are a lazy mom or dad. Ask a friend or relative to watch your baby for a few hours. Go to the park, a quiet café, or somewhere restful. If you can afford to hire help, even if it's only for a few hours each week, then do it.

CHILDREN CAUSE CHAOS

Children are noisy and messy, which can be hard to cope with if you're an HSP who dislikes loud sounds and chaotic environments. HSPs often need more sleep than the average person to feel at their best. Unfortunately, new parents are usually worn out from caring for their new baby.

If you are a perfectionist with high housekeeping standards, give yourself permission to lower them, at least for a while. It isn't realistic to aim for a pristine home with a baby or a young child. If you can afford it, consider hiring a housekeeper for a couple of hours per week.

Teach your child to take responsibility for their belongings from an early age. As soon as they are old enough to help clean up, encourage them to pick up their toys and lend a hand with the housework. Give them lots of praise when they keep their room neat and clean.

Children learn how to cope with their stress by watching your behavior. Minor crises and problems are an inevitable part of parenting, but you can promote a calm atmosphere at home and reduce the chaos.

Try these ideas:

Simplify your family's routine. If you stick to the same daily or weekly routine, you'll free up mental energy you would otherwise have spent planning the day ahead. Put a family calendar on the fridge, so everyone knows what is happening each day.

Avoid overscheduling activities. It may seem like other parents fill up their children's calendars, but this doesn't mean you have to follow suit. There's nothing wrong with giving your child some unstructured time or letting them feel bored. Boredom encourages self-sufficiency and creativity; your child will learn that sometimes they have to entertain themselves.

Make meditation and mindfulness family activities. Young children can learn to be mindful. If you teach them the basic principles early, they will grow up knowing how to cope with stressful situations.

Grounding exercises are a good place to start. Teach your child that when they feel very upset or angry and want to calm down, they should look for one thing they can see, one thing they can hear, one thing they can touch, one thing they can smell, and one thing they can taste.

Children can also learn breathing exercises. Help them practice breathing in through their nose and out through their mouth. Encourage them to use their imagination by pretending that they are breathing in a red mist and exhaling cool blue air. The next time you sense that they are about to have a tantrum, start the breathing exercise and ask them to copy you.

You can also use meal and snack times to encourage mindfulness. Ask your child how their food tastes and what it feels like on their tongue. Help them practice getting in tune with their bodies. This has an additional benefit—when they are ill or injured, they will probably be better than most children at describing their symptoms.

Limit overstimulating toys, games, and media. Watching an occasional movie or playing a few video games won't harm your child, but too much screen time or loud, flashy toys can leave them (and you!) overstimulated and irritable. Encourage quieter activities like crafts and reading instead, balanced with daily physical exercise, preferably outdoors.

Teach your child how to talk about their feelings and resolve conflict. As soon as they are capable of having meaningful conversations, teach your child how to talk about their feelings, express what they want in a constructive way, and come up with potential solutions to a problem.

For example, if your child seems angry, ask them, "Can you tell me how you're feeling inside?" Ask them to tell you what feeling angry is like. Then ask them what they want to happen next. Having understood what they are feeling and why, you can then explain what will happen next. If you can follow one of their suggestions, great! If not, thank them for telling you what they want, and then tell them why it's not possible. Your aim is to help them feel understood and respected, even if you can't give them what they want.

If you have two or more children, teach them how to resolve their differences. If they are mature enough to stay quiet when someone else is speaking, sit them down to-gether the next time they have a fight. Ask both of them to tell you in their own words what happened, what they are thinking, and what they are feeling. Listen carefully and paraphrase what they say to check that you've understood them.

When you have an overview of the situation, tell them that you are willing to resolve the issue for them, but you'd like them to come to an agreement themselves. Give them a few minutes alone to decide what they need to do; perhaps one or both needs to apologize, maybe they need to agree to disagree, or they might need to compromise. When you come back into the room, ask them what they've decided.

Sometimes, you'll still need to use your authority as a parent to tell them what happens next, but giving your children a chance to calm down and work together can pay off. If they come to a resolution by themselves, praise them for their maturity and emotional intelligence.

BECOMING A PARENT CAN TRIGGER OLD EMOTIONAL WOUNDS AND INSECURITIES

Raising children often makes us reflect on our childhoods, for better and for worse. For example, seeing your child being bullied can be even more painful if you were victim-ized at school. As an HSP, it's all too easy for you to recall painful memories. Incidents you may have suppressed for many years could suddenly come to the surface.

Becoming a mom or dad can also put your own par-ents' behaviors in a new light. For instance, if you always encourage your child to open up about how they are feeling, it may suddenly occur to you that your mother's cold parenting style could have caused you a lot of problems. This type of realization can bring up a lot of anger and unresolved grievances.

You may need to reparent yourself or see a therapist to work through difficult memories. Try keeping a journal to record thoughts and feelings as they pop up. HSPs are great at self-analysis, so use this strength to your advantage.

OTHER PEOPLE MAY CRITICIZE YOUR PARENTING SKILLS

When you're a parent, it feels like everyone you know has an opinion on everything you do, from what you feed your kids to how much time they spend watching TV. Some of this criticism will come from people you might think would know better—other parents. Although it's hard to remember when someone else's comments bring you down, try to bear in mind that the most critical, judgmental parents are often the most insecure.

On the bright side, your sensitive, empathetic personality will help you develop meaningful relationships with other struggling parents. As an HSP, you prefer to understand, rather than judge, your fellow moms and dads. Be honest about the reality of parenting, and others will probably share their stories too.

Parenting and child "experts" also have strong opinions about the best way to raise children. If you go to your local bookstore, you'll find lots of parenting books written by highly-qualified people. The problem is that they don't always agree with one another. It's hard to know whom to trust.

As long as you parent from a place of love and empathy—which, as an HSP, comes naturally to you—and adapt your approach to your child's needs and personality, you don't need to worry too much about the finer details like sleep schedules or whether they eat enough green vegetables. Follow a parenting book if you like, but don't despair if the advice doesn't quite fit your family. Babies are individuals, and they aren't interested in sticking to any rulebook!

SOCIALIZING WITH OTHER PARENTS CAN BE STRESSFUL

Spending time with other new parents can be helpful when your child is young. If you are a stay-at-home parent, going to parent and baby or parent and toddler groups can be a precious opportunity for adult conversation. However, if you are an introverted HSP, meeting new people and supervising your child as they play with their new friends can be emotionally draining.

Honor your needs. Just because you now have a child doesn't mean you have to become a social butterfly. Don't force yourself to attend a group if you don't like the atmosphere. Some parents' groups can be cliquey and unwelcoming; if you don't like the first or second group you find, try another. When you meet someone you like, ask them whether they'd like to meet up outside the group. You can also connect with other parents online via parenting forums or Facebook groups.

BECOMING A PARENT CAN MAKE YOU FEEL AS THOUGH YOU'RE LOSING YOUR IDENTITY

Before your child was born, you probably had lots of different identities. For example, perhaps you were an employee, a friend, a spouse, a volunteer, and a member of your local book club. Suddenly, with a new baby to look after, it may seem as though your world has literally shrunk overnight. As an HSP, routine probably helps you feel secure and grounded, so these changes can be very unsettling.

Find ways of keeping in touch with those things that are important to you, even if all your time is now taken up with family responsibilities. For example, you might not be able to attend a weekly book club, but you could try to enjoy reading a few pages of a book every day. Or perhaps you don't have time to volunteer with a charity on Sunday mornings anymore, but you could still stay up to date with their activities and participate in a single fundraising event or online meeting.

DISCIPLINING YOUR CHILD CAN MAKE YOU FEEL GUILTY

Not many parents enjoy disciplining their child, but highly sensitive parents are especially likely to feel guilty about imposing consequences for bad behavior because they are afraid of causing their child any kind of emotional harm or distress. However, consistent discipline is essential. Kids need to learn the difference between right and wrong, and they also need to understand that their behavior has consequences for other people.

Shouting at a child, particularly if they are sensitive, will often backfire. They will probably obey you. However, their obedience will probably come from a place of fear rather than respect. Shouting and barking orders will stress you out too, so no one wins. Only raise your voice if your child is in danger or if you're in a noisy place and need to make yourself heard.

Talk about logical consequences instead of making threats. For example, instead of saying, "If you don't stop whining, you're going into time out!" say, "You have a choice. You can either use a normal tone of voice and stop complaining, or you can sit by yourself in your room until you're ready to join everyone else again." Be matter of fact, not emotional. You also need to remain consistent. If your child is allowed to get away with bad behavior once, they will learn that it's OK and keep trying to push your boundaries.

Most children want to please their parents and respond well to positive reinforcement. When they behave well, praise them. If you want to change a long-term behavior, such as tidying their room every day, try using reward charts to track their progress. However, giving too many rewards can lead to a sense of entitlement. If your child learns that they can expect a payoff every time they do something right, they may carry this attitude into adolescence and adulthood. As a general rule, show your appreciation via praise rather than material possessions. Encourage your child to help out and be kind to others simply because it's the right thing to do.

Make sure you and your partner agree when it comes to household rules and discipline. Otherwise, your child may come to see one of you as the "fun parent" and the other as the "strict parent," which can lead to resentment. You need to present a united front, or your child may attempt to play you off against one another.

If you're tired of saying "no" all day, get creative with your wording while still upholding boundaries and rules. For example, let's say your child wants to watch TV, but their room is a mess. Instead of saying, "No, you need to put your toys away first," you could say, "Of course you can watch TV—when you've finished cleaning up your room." You are making the same request, just in a friendlier way.

Finally, distraction can be a useful discipline technique because it can stop bad behavior before it starts. It's especially effective for younger children. For example, if your toddler starts drawing on the table, quickly pull out a drawing pad and, without saying a word, set them on the floor and encourage them to use the pad. This approach teaches your child appropriate behavior with no conflict.

POSTNATAL DEPRESSION & POSTPARTUM PSYCHOSIS: KNOW THE SIGNS

Becoming a parent is a life-changing event, and it's normal to feel overwhelmed as you learn how to care for your new son or daughter. If you've given birth, your body might take weeks or even months to recover. Although there is no conclusive scientific evidence, highly sensitive people may be more vulnerable to postnatal depression because they are easily affected by major changes to their routines and relationships.

Most women feel low, worried, or tearful for the first week or so after giving birth. This is called "baby blues." However, if the baby blues haven't lifted after a couple of weeks, you could have postnatal depression.

The symptoms of postnatal depression include:

- Feeling tearful
- Feeling helpless
- Loss of interest in activities you used to enjoy
- A feeling that you can't bond with your baby
- Disturbing thoughts, such as thoughts of harming yourself or the baby
- Social withdrawal

You might need psychotherapy, medication, or both if you have postnatal depression. Some women also find support groups helpful. If you're worried that your baby will be taken away, rest assured that child protection services are very reluctant to separate families. Even if you have to go to a hospital for treatment, it's always a last resort.

It's quite common—more than 10% of mothers feel depressed in the first year following birth—so your doctor will know how to support you. It can also affect fathers and partners. It's important to get help quickly because, in rare cases, it can be a sign of postpartum psychosis, a serious mental illness that requires prompt treatment.

IF YOUR CHILD IS AN HSP

If you have a highly sensitive child, you can offer them a great gift—understanding. You have first-hand experience of life as an HSP, and you'll be able to share tips and strategies that you know to be helpful.

Here are some ways to help them thrive:

Give them a safe, private space. A highly sensitive child needs a soothing environment that allows them to seek privacy when they need it. Teach them that it's OK to retreat to their room for a while when they feel overstimulated. Choose soft lighting, soothing colors, and light fabrics when you decorate their room. Some HSP children benefit from sleeping with a weighted blanket.

Teach them that it's OK to be different. There's no getting around it, as a sensitive child, your son or daughter will meet many people who can't understand them. They may have to deal with bullying and social rejection. That's why it's important to teach them two things: First, that everyone has their own special traits and talents, and second, that they must get help if others hurt them.

Tell them about your experiences as a young HSP and how you dealt with setbacks. Knowing that you have faced similar problems can inspire them to do the same.

Encourage them to express their feelings in a healthy way. Most children enjoy being creative, and art, music, and writing can be good outlets for HSPs of all ages. Young

HSPs may not be able to express their feelings verbally, but they might be able to draw or paint their emotions. You can then use their creation as a starting point for talking about feelings. For example, you might say, "Wow, there's a lot of red in this painting! Is the red a good feeling or a difficult feeling?"

Let them fail. You may be tempted to step in and help whenever your child is having difficulty with their homework, tying their shoes, or learning how to work a new toy. But children need to understand that failure and frustration are a normal part of life. If they ask you for help before trying to solve a problem themselves, encourage them to keep trying for a while longer.

Don't give them preferential treatment. If you have other children, you may realize that you can relate to your HSP child better than the others. It's normal; most parents, even if they don't admit it to themselves or others, have a favorite child. However, you need to be careful not to let your feelings show. This is especially difficult if your HSP child is needy. Be honest about the amount of time you spend with each of your children.

Get professional help if your child is struggling. Taking your child to see a therapist or psychologist doesn't make you a bad parent. It means you are taking your son or daughter's welfare seriously, which makes you an excellent mom or dad. It's OK to acknowledge that you don't have all the knowledge and skills you need to raise a highly sensitive child, even if you are an HSP too. Try to find a mental health professional who has experience working with sensitive children.

CHAPTER 10:

WHY HSPS BENEFIT FROM SOCIAL MEDIA DETOXES

The average American adult spends more than two hours per day on social media, and most of us will spend the equivalent of several years online (but not for work or school) during our lifetimes.

Social media is a lot of fun. It's great for keeping up with friends and family, and some people upload genuinely helpful, uplifting content. There are also some wonderful HSP support groups you can use to meet people who can relate to your experiences.

However, too much social media can be draining, or even dangerous, for sensitive people. In this chapter, you'll learn why HSPs need to be careful about their social media use, and how a social media detox can reduce your stress and anxiety while improving your relationships.

First, let's review the reasons why social media can be a minefield for HSPs.

SOCIAL MEDIA CAN BE OVERSTIMULATING

There is an infinite number of posts, photos, videos, and gifs online. It can be hard to tune out the noise and focus on the content that enriches your life. Social media platforms use algorithms to show you posts and ads that align with your interests, which keeps you hooked in. Although it isn't yet formally recognized as a disorder, technology addiction—which includes internet dependency—is increasingly common. Cutting back on your social media usage can lower your risk.

SOCIAL MEDIA CAN BE TOXIC

You've probably seen people make passive-aggressive remarks and start arguments online. Even if you don't get involved in any heated discussions, watching others tear each other apart on social media can make you feel tired, upset, and anxious. Spending too much time watching people arguing on the internet can damage your faith in humanity.

SOCIAL MEDIA ENCOURAGES US TO COMPARE OURSELVES TO OTHERS

If you're an introverted HSP, scrolling through photos of people enjoying raucous parties with their friends can make you fear that you're missing out. As an HSP, you've probably been told many times that you need to "do more" or "get out more," and social media can reinforce that message. Although you know that you prefer to socialize with only one or two people, too much time on Instagram or Facebook can plant seeds of self-doubt.

Social media can feel like a popularity contest. It's easy to become insecure about the number of shares or likes your posts get or how many people are following you. If you are the type of person who fears rejection, you may become preoccupied with how much attention you get compared to everyone else. Perhaps you've caught yourself wondering why someone didn't respond to one of your posts or felt upset because someone unfollowed you with no explanation.

SOCIAL MEDIA CAN TAKE UP VALUABLE TIME YOU COULD BE USING FOR SELF-CARE

How many times have you said to yourself, "I'll just spend 10 minutes on Facebook," and then suddenly realized that an hour has gone by? Ask yourself this: What else could you be doing with that time? If you are an HSP who leads a busy life, you probably don't have enough time for rest and relaxation. Cutting back on social media can free up more space for activities that will improve your mental, physical, and spiritual health.

SOCIAL MEDIA CAN GIVE YOU A FALSE SENSE OF INTIMACY AND CONNECTION

Exchanging comments, "Likes," and retweets is a safe way to "talk" to people without having to make conversation or deal with their emotions face to face, which makes it appealing for HSPs who get overwhelmed in social situations.

There's nothing wrong with online friendships or shar-ing stories with people you wouldn't have a chance to meet in your everyday life, but it isn't a substitute for face to face friends. And if you aren't careful, you can become so wrapped up on your online life that you neglect your loved ones.

SOCIAL MEDIA OFTEN HIGHLIGHTS EVERYTHING THAT'S GOING WRONG IN THE WORLD

It's good to keep up to date with current affairs, but watch-ing and reading upsetting, anxiety-inducing news stories can quickly zap your emotional energy. You may feel guilty that you are relatively blessed compared to other people and that you shouldn't feel bad about your life. While it's good to feel grateful for what you have, this kind of guilt is destructive.

HOW TO DO YOUR FIRST SOCIAL MEDIA DETOX

A one-week social media detox gives you a chance to step away from your screen. You don't need to stop using your favorite sites forever. This challenge is to help you use social media in a more mindful way, not to cut yourself off from friends and family.

Here's your goal: Over the next 7 days, you are going to stay away from all forms of social media. This includes forums and message boards, along with Facebook, Twitter, and Instagram.

Here's how to make it a little easier:

PLAN YOUR WEEK

Decide what you're going to do in the time you'd usually spend online. Plan some activities to keep you occupied. Put together a list of distractions you can turn to when you feel compelled to check your social media accounts. The more anxious you feel about stepping away from your phone, the more you'll benefit from a schedule. Here are a few ideas:

- Read a book or magazine
- Go for a long walk with your partner or a good friend and have a deep conversation
- Visit a museum or art gallery
- Enjoy some extra sleep
- Catch up with chores or DIY projects
- Do a creative activity or craft
- Meditate
- Cook or bake something you've never tried before
- Play with your pet or with your children
- Phone a friend you haven't seen for a while and catch up
- Play a board game
- Go to a local community event
- Volunteer for a cause you care about

LET YOUR FRIENDS AND FAMILY KNOW WHAT YOU'RE DOING

If you often interact with friends and family on social media, they might be worried if you suddenly disappear.

Explain that you're doing a detox. Tell them that if they want to talk to you, they'll need to call.

KEEP YOUR PHONE IN A DIFFERENT ROOM

During the first couple of days, put your phone far out of reach. In theory, you could simply get up to retrieve it, but the distance will act as a buffer. For example, if it takes you a few seconds to get up from the couch in the living room and go to your bedroom, that gives you some time to think about what you are doing and make a better choice.

ASK SOMEONE TO HOLD YOU ACCOUNTABLE

Check in with a friend every evening by phone or text. Choose someone who will give you some encouragement when things get tough. If you have a deep-seated addiction, let a trusted friend or relative change the passwords to your accounts and hand them over only when the week comes to an end. Why not ask one of your friends to do a detox too? Everyone could benefit from spending less time online, whether they are an HSP or not.

TRY NOT TO USE ONLINE GAMING OR OTHER WEBSITES AS A REPLACEMENT FOR SOCIAL MEDIA

Technically, you wouldn't be cheating if you chose to do something else online instead of spending time on social media. However, you wouldn't enjoy the benefits that come with investing in your offline life. Try to stay away from your phone or computer screen as much as possible. Put a reminder on your lock screen

Change your wallpaper to something that reminds you of your mission and helps you avoid giving in to temptation. For example, you could create a background that says, "Do you really need to look at social media?" or "Remember, this week you're not on Facebook!"

PLAN A REWARD

Before you start your detox, pick out a small reward in advance. When the week is over, give yourself lots of praise. You've done something very few people can manage, and you should feel proud.

WHAT TO DO IF YOU SLIP UP

If temptation gets the better of you, don't beat yourself up. Take a few deep breaths, close your browser or app, and put some distance between you and your device. Then just pick up where you left off. There's no need to start from Day 1 if you have a slipup on Day 6, for example (although you can if you like).

See every setback as a great opportunity to learn something about yourself. Ask yourself how you were feeling and what you were thinking immediately before you reached for your phone. Was it just an automatic action, or was something else going on?

Perhaps you had an argument with your partner and wanted to distract yourself by scrolling Instagram. Think about ways you could meet your emotional needs without social media. Maybe you could try a mindfulness exercise, a vigorous workout, or calling a friend to make yourself feel better the next time you get upset.

REFLECT ON YOUR EXPERIENCE

Many people find the first few days of a social media detox very difficult, but by the end of the week, they realize that cutting back leaves them with more time and mental energy. You might be amazed by how much more you accomplish and how confident you feel when you make your "real" life a priority.

If you want to reinstall your social media apps and reactivate your accounts, consider making a few changes. For example, you could:

- Unfollow or delete accounts or connections that make you feel sad, anxious, or insecure.
- Place social media apps in a folder on your phone, not on your home screen, so you can't access them easily.
- Decide that you will only use social media to follow accounts or people you like, and not upload or post anything of your own.
- Install an app that limits how much time you spend on social media or even blocks it completely.
- Use only one social media platform.
- Choose to ignore sensationalist news articles on your social media feed unless it's been reposted or shared from a reputable website.
- Choose only to respond to positive or neutral comments on your posts.

- Decide that you won't multitask when browsing social media. For example, try not to use Facebook when eating dinner or scroll through Instagram while chatting with your spouse or children.
- Think about your other digital habits. For example, do you spend too much time playing videogames or browsing online stores?
- Schedule regular social media detoxes. You could stay off social media every Sunday, for example, or repeat the 7-day detox every month.

Rethinking your relationship with social media could be one of the best things you'll ever do for your mental health. Try it for yourself!

CHAPTER 11:

HOW TO OVERCOME PERFECTIONISM & IMPOSTER SYNDROME

H SPs have extremely high standards for themselves in both their professional and personal lives. Sometimes, this perfectionism works in your favor, but other times it can leave you exhausted and burned out.

In this chapter, you'll learn how to tame excessive perfectionism. We'll also talk about Imposter Syndrome: why it often accompanies perfectionist traits, what causes it, how it can affect your life, and how to overcome it.

WHY ARE HSPS PERFECTIONISTS?

YOU FIND IT EASY TO IMAGINE WHAT YOUR IDEAL OUTCOME IS

Because you have a good imagination, you can conjure up a picture of what life could be like if everything went perfectly. On the plus side, having a vision of what you want can keep you focused on your goals. The downside is that when life doesn't live up to your expectations, the disappointment can be crushing. When you fix your sights on a desired outcome, you can be reluctant to pivot or change course.

YOU REMEMBER WHAT IT FEELS LIKE TO FAIL, AND WANT TO AVOID FEELING THAT WAY AGAIN

As someone who feels every emotion very strongly and who can easily recall significant events from the past, the mere thought of failure is painful. By pouring energy into a project, you may be trying to shield yourself against it, even if you know that failure is part of life.

OTHERS MAY HAVE OSTRACIZED YOU OR MADE YOU FEEL "WEIRD," SO IT ALWAYS FEELS AS THOUGH YOU HAVE SOMETHING TO PROVE

Many HSPs report feeling like an outsider from an early age. Some HSPs give up trying to win everyone else's acceptance and retreat into their own world. However, others take the opposite approach. They try to prove themselves worthy by becoming high achievers. Consciously or unconsciously, they think that achieving great things will help them fit in.

YOU ARE SENSITIVE TO TINY DETAILS

You know that small things can make a big difference. When you approach a project, you might quickly become hung up over tiny details that other people wouldn't notice.

YOU LIKE TO FEEL IN CONTROL

Being highly attuned to your environment can be overwhelming and scary. Fixating on a goal can give you a sense of control, which can make you feel less anxious—at least in the short term.

Your perfectionism may not be confined to the workplace. You can be a perfectionist when it comes to your hobbies, your appearance, your finances, housework, and even your relationships.

DOES PERFECTIONISM IMPROVE YOUR PERFORMANCE?

Psychologists have discovered that there are two types of perfectionism: Excellence-seeking perfectionism and failure-avoidance perfectionism.

If you're an excellence-seeking perfectionist, you're driven by a desire to be the very best. You have high standards for yourself and others. If you asked the average person what a "perfectionist" is like, they'd probably describe the excellence-seeking type.

Failure-avoidance perfectionism is very different. It's characterized by a desire to avoid failing or falling short of a goal at all costs. These perfectionists are less likely to gain any kind of enjoyment from their work because they are so concerned about messing it up.

Although some people credit their perfectionism for their success, most research shows that there is no link between either type of perfectionism and performance. You might believe that letting go of your perfectionist tendencies means your work will suffer, but it's unlikely.

On the other hand, the cost of excessive perfectionism is high. Perfectionists are often tired and feel like life is just one long series of crises and challenges. In extreme cases, they collapse under self-imposed pressure.

Perfectionism can also go hand in hand with procrastination. If you are afraid of criticism and failure, it may seem safer to avoid a task or project entirely than risk trying and failing. Unfortunately, this can lead to a different kind of self-criticism—when you hold yourself back, anxiety and depression can set in. HSPs in this position can feel trapped and stifled because they aren't venturing beyond their comfort zone.

HOW TO LET GO OF PERFECTIONISM

BUILD SELF-ACCEPTANCE AND SELF-COMPASSION

Self-acceptance is a powerful antidote to perfectionism. Accepting yourself doesn't mean giving up on your goals. Neither does it entail building an overly optimistic self-image. It means acknowledging that your worth as a human being does not depend on your achievements. To accept yourself is to understand and embrace what makes you unique.

Self-compassion is slightly different and complements self-acceptance. It means treating yourself with the kindness you would show to someone you love.

Imagine that your best friend is upset because she received a low mark on an essay or didn't get very good feedback on a project at work. What would you say to him or her? You'd probably honor your friend's feelings, point out that a single setback doesn't make them a failure, and reassure them that they'll do better in the future. You might encourage them to get help from people who could give them a few hints and tips, like a mentor at work or their professor.

Here are a few exercises and strategies that can help develop both self-compassion and self-acceptance:

Exercise #1: Loving-kindness meditation

Find a comfortable place to sit or lie down. Close your eyes and breathe deeply for a couple of minutes. Bring someone to mind that you love and care about, such as your partner or a close friend. Imagine sending them warm, loving rays of light. Say aloud, "I love you and accept you."

Swap your mental image of your loved one for an image of yourself. Picture yourself surrounded by an orb of white or yellow light. Say aloud, "I love and accept you." The first time you try this, your words may feel hollow, but if you do it every day, your self-compassion will grow.

Exercise #2: Give yourself a hug

Getting a hug from someone else feels great—and so does getting a hug from yourself! The next time you start attacking yourself, take a deep breath and wrap your arms around yourself. This will calm your nervous system and reduce your stress levels. Alternatively, put one hand over your heart and feel it beating.

Exercise #3: Spot patterns

Most of us feel kinder and more accepting of ourselves on some occasions than others. Try keeping a diary for a few days. When you feel unusually self-critical, write down the day, time, and what you were doing immediately before the negative thoughts and feelings kicked in. This notetaking can help you make positive changes.

Let's say that one morning, you start criticizing yourself about your career. Perhaps you begin to think negative, unhelpful thoughts like "I should be making more money" or "I should be in a management role by now." You write them down in your journal. After reflecting for a couple of minutes, you realize that a few moments ago, you saw an article about a very successful businessperson on your social media feed. Thinking about it further, you realize that this is a recurring pattern for you: you read about very accomplished people, start comparing yourself, and beat yourself up.

Having identified this pattern, you can decide what to do about it. This may mean avoiding the trigger, but that isn't always possible. In some cases, it's more helpful to reframe it as an opportunity to appreciate yourself or to feel inspired.

To continue with the example above, you could decide to limit the number of articles you read about very successful people. Alternatively, you could decide that whenever you start feeling insecure about your career, you will remind yourself of your professional achievements so far. Use your triggers as an opportunity for positive self-talk. In this case, you could say, "Yes, it's true that I haven't achieved everything I want to achieve yet. But my career is far from over. I trust that with time and effort, I can realize my full potential."

KEEP A LIST OF YOUR ACHIEVEMENTS

Perfectionists often overlook the things they've done well because they are so busy focusing on their mistakes. Avoid falling into this trap by keeping a written record of your triumphs. Try to write a few things down every week. Read through your list when you feel as though you aren't good enough.

If you are a perfectionist in your relationships, keep a record of all the compliments you receive. Make a note of all the good times you spend with the people you love. When you begin to doubt your social skills or the strength of your relationships, remind yourself that you have plenty of love in your life.

PRACTICE BEING "GOOD ENOUGH" NOT "THE VERY BEST"

Rather than trying to do everything to an exceptional standard, work out what "good enough" looks like, and use it as your guide. For example, let's say your boss has asked you to type up some notes from a recent meeting. If you wanted, you could spend hours polishing every sentence, but the notes are there to serve as a record of what happened at the meeting—they don't have to be a literary masterpiece. All you need to do is produce a clear, helpful guide to who said what.

DELIBERATELY DO (SMALL) THINGS BADLY

For example, if you tend to obsess over being on time, show up to a meeting or date several minutes late. Let yourself be fallible. You'll quickly learn that imperfection isn't the end of the world, and most people will forgive small mistakes.

REWARD YOURSELF WHEN THINGS GO WELL

Many perfectionists are reluctant to reward themselves for anything because they don't feel comfortable owning their success. Get out of this habit by choosing a reward before you even begin a project. It doesn't have to be anything big or expensive; it could be a new book, a trip to the movies, or lunch at your favorite restaurant.

PICTURE A REALISTIC WORST-CASE SCENARIO AND DECIDE HOW YOU WOULD DEAL WITH IT

Perfectionists often dwell on the "what ifs." They torment themselves by obsessing over worst-case scenarios. Because they usually believe they won't be able to handle a disaster or emergency, this rumination drives their stress levels even higher.

Although it will be scary at first, facing your fears—at least, in your imagination—can help.

Here's how to do it:

- Set aside 10 minutes for this exercise. Make sure you won't be disturbed.
- Close your eyes and picture a scenario that is worrying you. For example, suppose you are worried that you will stutter or miss a key piece of information when giving a big presentation at work.

Imagine yourself standing up in front of everyone, talking as you click through your slides on a large screen.

- Now freeze the image in your mind. Take a couple of deep breaths.

- Imagine that the worst-case scenario happens. To continue with the presentation example, picture yourself losing your train of thought entirely, having a panic attack, or both. Imagine the long-term consequences, such as a negative appraisal from your manager.

- Praise yourself for making it this far through the exercise.

- Now imagine how you would handle the worst-case scenario. Imagine yourself taking charge of the situation. Who could you talk to? What techniques could you use to calm yourself down? If you had to deal with a big disappointment, such as the loss of a friendship or job opportunity, how would you cope?

- Your first response might be "I couldn't cope!" or "There's nothing that could make the situation better!" But when you take a closer look at a problem, there is almost always a solution—or at least a way to deal with the fallout. Sometimes, adversity can make us stronger and more resilient. The bottom line is this: very few worst-case scenarios are truly fatal. Most of the time, we create our own suffering by dwelling on frightening but remote possibilities.

A variation on this technique is to think about times at which you had to cope with a major setback. Even if you wish you had acted differently, the very fact you are reading this proves that you survived.

READ BIOGRAPHIES OF SUCCESSFUL PEOPLE

Very few successful people have avoided making mistakes. Read up on a famous person you admire. There's a good chance they've made a few blunders, but you probably don't hold that against them. Why not extend yourself the same grace?

HELP OTHER PEOPLE

It's difficult to believe that you have no worth as a human being when you make a positive difference to others. Helping those in need can also help you gain a sense of perspective. Your pain is real and valid, but sometimes, helping people in a worse position can give you a renewed sense of gratitude that makes your failures seem less important.

IMPOSTER SYNDROME: THE COUSIN OF PERFECTIONISM

Imposter Syndrome isn't a medical diagnosis, but it's a recognized psychological phenomenon. People with Imposter Syndrome are often highly accomplished and competent, but they don't accept and enjoy their own success. They have a constant fear of being "found out" or exposed as a fraud. This makes them susceptible to anxiety and depression. If they refuse to believe or accept compliments and praise, people with Imposter Syndrome can inadvertently damage their relationships. Therefore, it's a good idea to overcome it.

WHAT ARE THE SIGNS THAT YOU HAVE IMPOSTER SYNDROME?

- Difficulty accepting sincere compliments and credit for a job well done
- Feelings of deep shame when you make a mistake
- Reluctance to try anything new in case you fail
- Reluctance to ask for help because you think you should be able to handle everything alone
- An obsession with training and professional development; you worry that you'll never truly become an expert in your field
- A feeling that you don't "have a right" to be in your job or to be given recognition for your work
- A tendency to attribute your successes to luck instead of hard work
- Procrastinating or putting off tasks because you're afraid that you won't be able to do them
- A tendency to feel depressed, anxious, or both
- A tendency to obsess over mistakes, even if they happened months or years ago
- Devaluing your worth; for example, perhaps you don't ask for the salary you truly deserve or ask for a fair price for your work
- Refusal to acknowledge your expertise, even if you've earned qualifications or worked in your field for a long time

The researchers who first described Imposter Syndrome initially thought it only affected women because girls are usually socialized to be more modest than boys. However, later studies showed that men can also suffer from Imposter Syndrome.

Why Do HSPs Feel Like Imposters?

As a highly sensitive child, your parents and teachers might not have known how best to encourage and support you. Some days they might have given you a lot of praise, but on other occasions, they might have become frustrated and critical. These mixed messages can leave you with a shaky self-image; you aren't sure whether you're good enough.

Imposter Syndrome goes hand-in-hand with perfectionism. Both are based on a fear of failure and a desire to develop self-worth. Most of the tips for overcoming perfectionism are also helpful for Imposter Syndrome, but there are a few additional strategies you might like to try.

Strategies for Beating Imposter Syndrome

Reach Out When You Need Help

People with Imposter Syndrome often pride themselves on being able to find the answers to their problems. This is a great quality, but you'll save a lot of time and stress by approaching someone who already has enough experience or expertise to point you in the right direction. Be brave enough to admit that you feel overwhelmed. There's a good chance that those around you also feel incompetent or like imposters some of the time.

In a healthy workplace or college, people can tell their colleagues and supervisors when they're struggling. If you work or study in an environment that punishes people who ask for help, maybe it's time to think about moving on.

BEFORE COMPARING YOURSELF TO OTHERS, REMEMBER THAT YOU DON'T KNOW THEIR LIFE STORY

Have you ever envied someone, only to later find out that they are secretly fighting serious problems or have a much more difficult life than you could have imagined? From the outside, some people appear to "have it all together." In reality, nobody has a perfect life. Yes, some people enjoy more comforts and better luck than others, but everyone has their share of problems and disappointments. You may be surprised to learn that someone might envy you!

ASK SOMEONE YOU RESPECT WHETHER THEY'VE SUFFERED FROM IMPOSTER SYNDROME

If you have a successful mentor or loved one in your life, tell them that you've been reading up on Imposter Syndrome. Ask them if the signs sound familiar. They can probably relate to your struggles and might be able to share some useful tips with you.

ASK FOR CRITICISM

If you can learn to tolerate negative feedback, you'll be considerably less anxious about making mistakes. Start by asking a trusted friend, colleague, or relative for honest feedback. Start with a low-stakes project or task. For example, before you send an email at work, you could ask a colleague to suggest any edits or rewrites.

Bear in mind that if you have reacted badly to criticism in the past, people might be hesitant to offer honest feedback. Be transparent. Tell them that you've realized how important feedback is and that although it's been hard for you to stomach criticism in the past, you want to teach yourself how to cope with it. Tell the other person that you value their opinion and would be very grateful for their help. Thank them graciously for their criticism, even if you don't agree with everything they say.

TRY ON THE IDENTITY OF "TEAM PLAYER"

Not many people can do their best work in isolation. We've all heard stories of geniuses who work alone, but most high achievers know the power of collaboration. Consider the possibility that you've become too attached to an ideal self who is entirely self-sufficient. Try imagining yourself as a highly competent, successful person who not only realizes their potential but also helps other people reach theirs. Some people find they are less likely to feel like imposters when they are part of a successful team.

REMEMBER THAT THE REFINING PROCESS IS PART OF ANY PROJECT

The first few ideas you have at the beginning of a project probably won't be your best. That's normal. Most people

have to redesign or refine their work. Try to welcome your
bad ideas; they are simply the first steps to success.

WHEN TO SEEK PROFESSIONAL HELP

If the tips in this chapter don't help, and you are still plagued
by perfectionism and Imposter Syndrome, consider seeing
a therapist. Some people have destructive beliefs that are so
deeply engrained that they need a professional to identify
and correct them. These problems can be linked to other
serious problems, such as childhood trauma or abuse. Therapy isn't easy, but it's worth the time and investment; it can
make all the difference between surviving and thriving.

CONCLUSION

Congratulations on taking the first step forward on your journey as an HSP! When you picked up this book, you probably felt somewhat nervous or perhaps even skeptical. That's completely normal—not many HSPs know that their personality type has a name and that there are millions of others out there who share their experiences.

Now that you understand what it really means to be an HSP, you will see yourself and your past in a new light. This paves the way to self-acceptance, which is one of the most precious gifts of all. No longer will you wonder why some people and places have such a dramatic effect on you, and no longer will you feel helpless in the face of your own emotions.

Remember that personal growth is a lifelong endeavor. Go at your own pace. For example, you may wish to focus on learning to cleanse yourself of negative energy first before re-evaluating your relationships. Just like any other skill, self-mastery becomes easier over time.

May your journey be fulfilling and joyous!

THANKS FOR READING!

I hope this book has helped you come to terms with your needs as an HSP and that you have enjoyed reading it as much as I enjoyed writing it!

It would mean a lot to me if you left an Amazon review—I will reply to all questions!

Please visit www.pristinepublish.com/hspreview to leave a review.

Be sure to check out my email list, where I am constantly adding tons of value.

The best way to get on it currently is by visiting www.pristinepublish.com/empathbonus and entering your email.

Here I'll provide actionable information that aims to improve your enjoyment of life.

I'll update you on my latest books and I'll even send free e-books that I think you'll find useful.

Kindest regards,

Also by
Judy Dyer

Grasp a better understanding of your gift and how you can embrace every part of it so that your life is enriched day by day.

Visit: www.pristinepublish.com/judy

REFERENCES

American Psychiatric Association. (2013). *DSM-V.*

Anderson, J. (2018). *Is Anxiety a Common Symptom in Gluten Disorders?*

Anxieties.com. (n.d.) *STEP 4: Practice Your Breathing Skills.*

Aron, E. (2013). *How Do You Recognize an HSP?*

Aron, E. (2018). *FAQ.*

Aron, E. (n.d.). *FAQ.*

Bjelland, J. (2018). *Careers/Jobs for the Highly Sensitive Person.*

Borchard, T.J. (2019). *4 Strategies to Foster Self-Compassion.*

Brandt, A. (2015). *What to Do When Your Emotions Overwhelm You.*

BroadbandSearch. (2020). *Average Time Spent Daily on Social Media.*

Clusters of Inspiration. (2016). *EQ meets HSP: Emotional Intelligence and the Highly Sensitive Person.*

Hunt, M.G., Marx, R., Lipson, C., & Young, J. (2018). No More FOMO: Limiting Social Media Decreases Loneliness and Depression. *Journal of Social and Clinical Psychology.*

Kruger, P. (n.d.). *The Anxious Parent.*

Lee, K. (2019). *Natural and Logical Consequences.*

Martin, S. (2019). *Highly Sensitive People and Perfectionism.*

McNamara, E. (2020). *Imposter Syndrome is Real.*

McQuillan, K. (2019). *What it's like to parent when you're a Highly Sensitive Person.*

Mind Tools. (n.d.) *Managing Highly Sensitive People.*

Monster-Peters, K. (2017). *My 27 Best Self-Care Tools, Tips, and Techniques for Highly Sensitive Parents.*

Newman, S. (2016). *How Highly Sensitive People Can Shield Themselves From Negativity.*

Nielsen. (2018). *Time Flies: U.S. Adults Now Spend Nearly Half A Day Interacting With Media.*

O'Laughlan, K. (n.d.) *HSPs and Depression.*

O'Laughlan, K. (n.d.) *Jobs and Careers for Highly Sensitive Persons.*

Orloff, J. (2017). *The Differences Between Highly Sensitive People and Empaths.*

Smit, A.W. (n.d.) *10 must-know misconceptions about (high) sensitive people.*

Solo, A. (2018). *The 7 Best Careers for a Highly Sensitive Person.*

Swider, B., Harari, D., Breidenthal, A.P., & Bujold Steed, L. (2018). *The Pros and Cons of Perfectionism, According to Research.*

Tartakovsky, M. (2018). *Therapists Spill: 12 Ways to Accept Yourself.*

Tartakovsky, M. (2018). *6 Ways to Start Practicing Self-Compassion — Even If You Believe You're Undeserving.*

Top10HomeRemedies. (n.d.) *How to Remove Negative Energy from Your Home.*

Top10HomeRemedies. (2016). *10 Plants that Attract Positive Energy.*

Walter, L. (2011). *R.I.D.E. the Wave of Panic.*

Ward, D. (2012). *Coping with Anxiety as an HSP.*

Weir, K. (2013). *Feel like a fraud?*